Edward Eggleston, Alexandre Bida

Christ in Art

The Story of the Words and Acts of Jesus Christ

Edward Eggleston, Alexandre Bida

Christ in Art
The Story of the Words and Acts of Jesus Christ

ISBN/EAN: 9783743388826

Manufactured in Europe, USA, Canada, Australia, Japa

Cover: Foto ©Lupo / pixelio.de

Manufactured and distributed by brebook publishing software (www.brebook.com)

Edward Eggleston, Alexandre Bida

Christ in Art

Christ in Art:

THE STORY OF THE WORDS AND ACTS OF JESUS CHRIST, AS RELATED IN THE
LANGUAGE OF THE FOUR EVANGELISTS, ARRANGED IN ONE
CONTINUOUS NARRATIVE.

By EDWARD EGGLESTON, D.D.

Illustrated

WITH ONE HUNDRED FULL-PAGE PLATES ON STEEL AND WOOD,

EXECUTED BY BREND'AMOUR, OF DÜSSELDORF.

AFTER THE FAMOUS DESIGNS OF

ALEXANDER BIDA,

TOGETHER WITH NUMEROUS EXPOSITORY ENGRAVINGS IN THE TEXT

BY

AMERICAN ARTISTS.

NEW YORK:
J. B. FORD AND COMPANY.
1875.

PREFACE.

GREAT pains have been taken in the construction of this work, to give the narrative the roundness, unity, and fluency that are so essential to the interest and picturesqueness of the story, and to a conception of the life of the Lord Jesus in its oneness and consecutiveness. Without doubt the best way to study Christ is to read each of the Gospels in its unity. Supplementary to this the scholar is able to construct for himself, by a laborious study of learned works and a diligent comparison of the several Gospels, a conception of the life of Christ as a whole. It is to assist the general reader in forming such a conception that the present consolidation is made.

It is now two hundred and twenty years since the learned Dr. Lightfoot published his celebrated harmony of the four Gospels; and very many others have labored in this field during these two centuries. But the plan and purpose of the present work differs in some regards from all that have gone before. For this is not

iii

a harmony, properly so called. No endeavor has been made to reconcile apparent discrepancies. Where there were variations in the minor details of an incident as given in the Gospels, I have followed that which was the fullest and the most vivid. I might have gone further in piecing together the narratives, but this sort of patchwork has been often made at the expense of fluency and interest in the history. To have woven into the narrative all the varying phrases of the four historians, even at the expense of clearness and grammatical construction, would have been to sacrifice to a masoretic veneration for the letter of the sacred text the interest and usefulness of the work. All marginal readings, and all references to the several Gospels, and all marks of chapters and verses in the Gospels, have been carefully omitted, that the attention of the reader might never be diverted from the narrative itself, and that the picture of Christ's life might be presented with that unbroken continuity to which we are accustomed in reading modern books. The preface to Luke, as pertaining to but one Gospel, and the two genealogies, have been omitted: since, however valuable they may be in their places, they would not help, but rather hinder, the purpose of this compilation. The present arrangement, therefore, is in the exact words of the authorized version of the Gospels; there is nothing added, nothing changed. But it makes no pretension to include every word of all the Gospels. It is better to be useful than ingenious.

The order of time is chiefly that marked out by Dr. Ellicott in his Hulsean Lectures. In minor arrangements and adaptations of the text much assistance has been derived from an anonymous Diatesseron published in Oxford in 1837.

I am fully aware that the principal attraction of the book is not the part which fell to my share, but the illustrations after Alexandre Bida's magnificent designs. The artist's pencil has hardly ever told THE STORY so effectively. To these the publishers have added a series of exegetical illustrations that serve exceedingly well to explain those portions of the narrative which refer to Oriental customs.

I sincerely hope that these pages may contribute something to a better comprehension of the life of the Son of Man, who "came not into the world to condemn the world, but that the world through him might be saved."

E. E.

November, 1874.

vi   THE CHRIST.

Contents.

CONTENTS.

Illustrations.

LIST OF ILLUSTRATIONS.

x

Christ in Art.

"SUFFER LITTLE CHILDREN TO COME UNTO ME."

INTRODUCTION.

THE ETERNAL WORD.

THE beginning of the Gospel of Jesus Christ the Son of God.

In the beginning was the Word, and the Word was with God, and the Word was God. The same was in the beginning with God. All things were *The Word eternal, divine, and the creator of the world.* made by him; and without him was not anything made that was made. In him was life; and the life was the light of men. And the light shineth in darkness; and the darkness comprehended it not.

There was a man sent from God, whose name was John. The same came for a witness, to bear witness of the Light, that all men through him might believe. He was not that Light, but was sent to bear witness *Christ, the true Light of the world.* of that Light. That was the true Light, which lighteth every man that cometh into the world. He was in the world, and the world was made by him, and the world knew him not. He came unto his own, and his own received him not. But as many as received him, to them gave he power to become the sons of God, even to them that believe on his name: which were born, not of blood, nor of the will of the flesh, nor of the will of man, but of God.

And the Word was made flesh, and dwelt among us, (and we beheld his glory, the glory as of the only begotten of the Father,) full of *The Word made flesh.* grace and truth. John bare witness of him, and cried, saying, "This was he of whom I spake, He that cometh after me is preferred before me: for he was before me. And of his fullness have all we received, and grace for grace. For the law was given by Moses, but grace and truth came by Jesus Christ. No man hath seen God at any time: the only-begotten Son, which is in the bosom of the Father, he hath declared him."

CHAPTER I.

THERE was in the days of Herod, the king of Judæa, a certain priest named Zacharias, of the course of Abia: and his wife was of the daughters of Aaron, and her name was Elisabeth. And they were The parentage of John. both righteous before God, walking in all the commandments and ordinances of the Lord blameless. And they had no child, because that Elisabeth was barren; and they both were now well stricken in years.

And it came to pass, that while he executed the priest's office before God in the order of his course, according to the custom of the priest's office, his lot was to burn incense when he went into the temple of the Lord. And the whole multitude of the people were praying without at the time of incense. And there appeared unto him an angel of the Lord, standing on the right side of the altar of incense. And when Zacharias saw him, he was troubled, and fear fell upon him. But the angel said unto him,

JEWISH PRIEST OFFERING INCENSE

"Fear not, Zacharias: for thy prayer is heard;
And thy wife Elisabeth shall bear thee a son,
And thou shalt call his name John.
And thou shalt have joy and gladness;
And many shall rejoice at his birth.
For he shall be great in the sight of the Lord,
And shall drink neither wine nor strong drink;
And he shall be filled with the Holy Ghost even from his mother's womb.
And many of the children of Israel shall he turn to the Lord their God.
And he shall go before him in the spirit and power of Elias,
To turn the hearts of the fathers to the children,
And the disobedient to the wisdom of the just;
To make ready a people prepared for the Lord."

And Zacharias said unto the angel, "Whereby shall I know this? for I am an old man, and my wife well stricken in years." And the angel answering said unto him, "I am Gabriel, that stand in the presence of God; and am sent to speak unto thee, and to show thee these glad tidings. And, behold, thou shalt be dumb, and not able to speak, until the day that these things shall be performed, because thou believest not my words, which shall be fulfilled in their season."

And the people waited for Zacharias, and marveled that he tarried so long in the temple. And when he came out, he could not speak unto them: and they perceived that he had seen a vision in the temple; for he beckoned unto them, and remained speechless. And it came to pass, that, as soon as the days of his ministration were accomplished, he departed to his own house.

And after those days his wife Elisabeth conceived, and hid herself five months, saying, "Thus hath the Lord dealt with me in the days wherein he looked on me, to take away my reproach among men."

And in the sixth month the angel Gabriel was sent from God unto a city of Galilee, named Nazareth, to a virgin espoused to a man whose name was Joseph, of the house of David; and the virgin's name was Mary. And the angel came in unto her, and said, "Hail, thou that art highly favored, the Lord is with thee: blessed art thou among women." And when she saw him, she was troubled at his saying, and cast in her mind what manner of salutation this should be. And the angel said unto her, "Fear not, Mary: for thou hast found favor with God. And, behold, thou shalt conceive in thy womb, and bring forth a son, and shalt call his name JESUS. He shall be great, and shall be called the Son of the Highest: and the Lord God shall give unto him the throne of his father David. And he shall reign over the house of Jacob forever; and of his kingdom there shall be no end."

The annunciation to Mary.

Then said Mary unto the angel, "How shall this be, seeing I know not a man?"

And the angel answered and said unto her, "The Holy Ghost shall come upon thee, and the power of the Highest shall overshadow thee: therefore also that holy thing which shall be born of thee shall be called the Son of God. And, behold, thy cousin Elisabeth, she hath also conceived a son in her old age; and this is the sixth month with her, who was called barren. For with God nothing shall be impossible."

And Mary said, "Behold the handmaid of the Lord; be it unto me according to thy word." And the angel departed from her.

And Mary arose in those days, and went into the hill country with haste, into a city of Juda; and entered into the house of Zacharias, and saluted Elisabeth. And it came to pass, that, when Elisabeth heard the salutation of Mary, the babe leaped in her womb; and Elisabeth was filled with the Holy Ghost: and she spake out with a loud voice, and said, —

Mary visits Elisabeth.

MARY'S VISIT TO ELIZABETH.

"Blessed art thou among women, and blessed is the fruit of thy womb. And whence is this to me, that the mother of my Lord should come to me? for, lo, as soon as the voice of thy salutation sounded in mine ears, the babe leaped in my womb for joy. And blessed is she that believed: for there shall be a performance of those things which were told her from the Lord."

And Mary said, —

> "My soul doth magnify the Lord,
> And my spirit hath rejoiced in God my Saviour.
> For he hath regarded the low estate of his handmaiden;
> For, behold, from henceforth all generations shall call me blessed.
> For he that is mighty hath done to me great things;
> And holy is his name.
> And his mercy is on them that fear him
> From generation to generation.
> He hath showed strength with his arm;
> He hath scattered the proud in the imagination of their hearts.
> He hath put down the mighty from their seats,
> And exalted them of low degree.
> He hath filled the hungry with good things;
> And the rich he hath sent empty away.
> He hath holpen his servant Israel,
> In remembrance of his mercy;
> As he spake to our fathers,
> To Abraham, and to his seed forever."

And Mary abode with her about three months, and returned to her own house.

Now Elisabeth's full time came that she should be delivered; and she brought forth a son. And her neighbors and her cousins heard how the Lord had showed great mercy upon her; and they rejoiced with her. And it came to pass, that on the eighth day they came to circumcise the child: and they called him Zacharias, after the name of his father.

The birth and circumcision of John.

And his mother answered and said, "Not so; but he shall be called John." And they said unto her, "There is none of thy kindred that is called by this name."

ANCIENT WRITING MATERIALS AND BOOKS.

And they made signs to his father, how he would have him called. And he asked for a writing-table, and wrote, saying, "His name is John." And they marveled all. And his mouth was opened immediately, and his tongue loosed, and he spake and praised God. And fear came on all that dwelt round about them: and all these sayings were

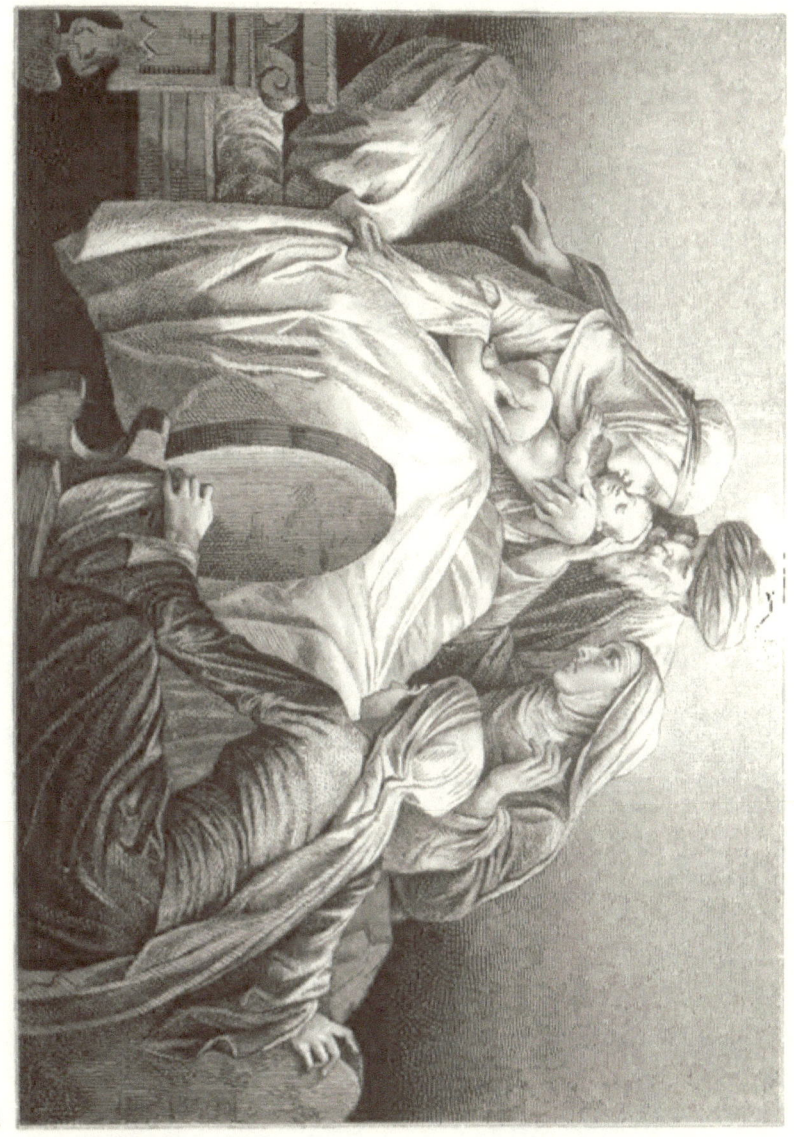

noised abroad throughout all the hill country of Judæa.   And all they that
heard them laid them up in their hearts, saying, "What manner of child
shall this be?"   And the hand of the Lord was with him.

*Zacharias proph-
esies.*

And his father Zacharias was filled with the Holy Ghost, and
prophesied, saying, —

> "Blessed be the Lord God of Israel;
> For he hath visited and redeemed his people,
> And hath raised up an horn of salvation for us
> In the house of his servant David;
> As he spake by the mouth of his holy prophets,
> Which have been since the world began:
> That we should be saved from our enemies,
> And from the hand of all that hate us;
> To perform the mercy promised to our fathers,
> And to remember his holy covenant,
> The oath which he sware to our father Abraham,
> That he would grant unto us,
> That we, being delivered out of the hand of our enemies,
> Might serve him without fear,
> In holiness and righteousness before him,
> All the days of our life.
> And thou, child, shalt be called the prophet of the Highest:
> For thou shalt go before the face of the Lord to prepare his ways;
> To give knowledge of salvation unto his people
> By the remission of their sins,
> Through the tender mercy of our God;
> Whereby the day-spring from on high hath visited us,
> To give light to them that sit in darkness and in the shadow of death,
> To guide our feet into the way of peace."

And the child grew and waxed strong in spirit, and was in the deserts till
the day of his showing unto Israel.

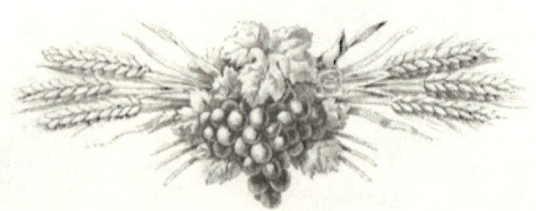

CHAPTER II.

OW the birth of Jesus Christ was on this wise: When as his mother Mary was espoused to Joseph, before they came together, she was found with child of the Holy Ghost. Then Joseph her husband, being a just man, and not willing to make her a public example, was minded to put her away privily.

Joseph's dream.

But while he thought on these things, behold, the angel of the Lord appeared unto him in a dream, saying, "Joseph, thou son of David, fear not to take unto thee Mary thy wife: for that which is conceived in her is of the Holy Ghost. And she shall bring forth a son, and thou shalt call his name JESUS: for he shall save his people from their sins."

Now all this was done, that it might be fulfilled which was spoken of the Lord by the prophet, saying, "Behold, a virgin shall be with child, and shall bring forth a son, and they shall call his name Emmanuel," which being interpreted is, "God with us."

Then Joseph, being raised from sleep, did as the angel of the Lord had bidden him, and took unto him his wife: and knew her not till she had brought forth her first-born son.

And it came to pass in those days, that there went out a decree from Cæsar Augustus, that all the world should be taxed. (And this taxing was first made when Cyrenius was governor of Syria.) And all went to be taxed, every one into his own city. And Joseph also went up from Galilee, out of the city of Nazareth, into Judæa, unto the city of David, which is called Bethlehem (because he was of the house and lineage of David), to be taxed with Mary his espoused wife, being great with child.

Joseph and Mary journey from Nazareth to Bethlehem.

And so it was that, while they were there, the days were accomplished that she should be delivered. And she brought forth her first-born son, and wrapped him in swaddling-clothes, and laid him in a manger; because there was no room for them in the inn.

The birth of Jesus.

And there were in the same country shepherds abiding in the field, keeping watch over their flock by night. And, lo, the angel of the Lord came

The angels and the shepherds. upon them, and the glory of the Lord shone round about them: and they were sore afraid. And the angel said unto them, "Fear not: for, behold, I bring you good tidings of great joy, which shall be to all people. For unto you is born this day in the city of David a Saviour, which is Christ the Lord. And this shall be a sign unto you: Ye shall find the babe wrapped in swaddling-clothes, lying in a manger."

And suddenly there was with the angel a multitude of the heavenly host praising God, and saying,

> " Glory to God in the highest,
> And on earth peace, good-will toward men."

And it came to pass, as the angels were gone away from them into heaven, the shepherds said one to another, " Let us now go even unto Bethlehem, and see this thing which is come to pass, which the Lord hath made known unto us."

And they came with haste, and found Mary, and Joseph, and the babe lying in a manger. And when they had seen it, they made known abroad

The shepherds find Jesus in a manger. the saying which was told them concerning this child. And all they that heard it wondered at those things which were told them by the shepherds. But Mary kept all these things, and pondered them in her heart. And the shepherds returned, glorifying and praising God for all the things that they had heard and seen, as it was told unto them.

And when eight days were accomplished for the circumcising of the

Jesus is circumcised. child, his name was called JESUS, which was so named of the angel before he was conceived in the womb.

And when the days of her purification according to the law of Moses were accomplished, they brought him to Jerusalem, to present him to the

Jesus is presented in the temple. Lord: (as it is written in the law of the Lord, " Every male that openeth the womb shall be called holy to the Lord ";) and to offer a sacrifice according to that which is said in the law of the Lord, " A pair of turtle-doves, or two young pigeons."

And, behold, there was a man in Jerusalem, whose name was Simeon; and the same man was just and devout, waiting for the consolation of

Simeon prophesies. Israel: and the Holy Ghost was upon him. And it was revealed unto him by the Holy Ghost, that he should not see death, before he had seen the Lord's Christ. And he came by the Spirit into the temple: and when the parents brought in the child Jesus, to do for him after the custom of the law, then took he him up in his arms, and blessed God, and said, " Lord, now lettest thou thy servant depart in peace, according to thy word: for mine eyes have seen thy salvation, which thou hast prepared before the face of all people; a light to lighten the Gentiles, and the glory of thy people Israel."

And Joseph and his mother marveled at those things which were spoken of him. And Simeon blessed them, and said unto Mary his mother, "Behold, this child is set for the fall and rising again of many in Israel; and for a sign which shall be spoken against; (yea, a sword shall pierce through thy own soul also;) that the thoughts of many hearts may be revealed."

And there was one Anna, a prophetess, the daughter of Phanuel, of the tribe of Aser: she was of a great age, and had lived with an husband seven years from her virginity; and she was a widow of about fourscore and four years, which departed not from the temple, but served God with fastings and prayers night and day. And she coming in that instant gave thanks likewise unto the Lord, and spake of him to all them that looked for redemption in Jerusalem.

Anna's prophecy.

D

CHAPTER III.

OW when Jesus was born in Bethlehem of Judæa in the days of Herod the king, behold, there came *Wise men from the East seek Jesus.* wise men from the East to Jerusalem, saying, "Where is he that is born King of the Jews? for we have seen his star in the east, and are come to worship him."

When Herod the king had heard these things, he was troubled, and all Jerusalem with him. And when he had gathered all the chief priests and scribes of the people together, he demanded of them where Christ should be born. And they said unto him, "In Bethlehem, of Judæa: for thus it is written by the prophet, 'And thou Bethlehem, in the land of Juda, art not the least among the princes of Juda: for out of thee shall come a Governor that shall rule my people Israel.'"

Then Herod, when he had privily called the wise men, inquired of them diligently what time the star appeared. And he sent them to Bethlehem, and said, "Go and search diligently for the young child; and when ye have found him, bring me word again, that I may come and worship him also." When they had heard the king, they departed; and, lo, the star, which they saw in the east, went before them, till it came and stood over where the young child was. When they saw the star, they rejoiced with exceeding great joy.

FRANKINCENSE AND MYRRH.

And when they were come into the house, they saw the young child with Mary his mother, and fell down, and worshiped *They find Jesus and worship him.* him; and when they had opened their treasures, they presented unto him gifts: gold, and frankincense, and myrrh. And being

THE DEPARTURE FOR EGYPT.

warned of God in a dream that they should not return to Herod, they departed into their own country another way.

And when they were departed, behold, the angel of the Lord appeareth to Joseph in a dream, saying, "Arise, and take the young child and his mother, and flee into Egypt, and be thou there until I bring thee word: for Herod will seek the young child to destroy him." *The flight into Egypt.* When he arose, he took the young child and his mother by night, and departed into Egypt: and was there until the death of Herod: that it might be fulfilled which was spoken of the Lord by the prophet, saying, "Out of Egypt have I called my Son."

Then Herod, when he saw that he was mocked of the wise men, was exceeding wroth, and sent forth, and slew all the children that were in Bethlehem, and in all the coasts thereof, from two years old and *The slaughter of the young children.* under, according to the time which he had diligently inquired of the wise men. Then was fulfilled that which was spoken by Jeremy the prophet, saying, "In Rama was there a voice heard, lamentation, and weeping, and great mourning, Rachel weeping for her children, and would not be comforted, because they are not."

But when Herod was dead, behold, an angel of the Lord appeareth in a dream to Joseph in Egypt, saying, "Arise, and take the young child and his mother, and go into the land of Israel: for they are *The return from Egypt.* dead which sought the young child's life."

And he arose, and took the young child and his mother, and came into the land of Israel. But when he heard that Archelaus did reign in Judæa in the room of his father Herod, he was afraid to go thither: notwithstanding, being warned of God in a dream, he turned aside into the parts of Galilee; and he came and dwelt in their own city, Nazareth: that it might be fulfilled which was spoken by the prophets, "He shall be called a Nazarene."

And the child grew, and waxed strong in spirit, filled with wisdom; and the grace of God was upon him.

Now his parents went to Jerusalem every year at the feast of the passover. And when he was twelve years old, they went up to Jerusalem after the custom of the feast. And when they had fulfilled the days, *Jesus converses with the doctors in the temple.* as they returned, the child Jesus tarried behind in Jerusalem; and Joseph and his mother knew not of it. But they, supposing him to have been in the company, went a day's journey; and they sought him among their kinsfolk and acquaintance. And when they found him not, they turned back again to Jerusalem, seeking him. And it came to pass, that after three days they found him in the temple, sitting in the midst of the doctors, both hearing them, and asking them questions. And all that heard him were astonished at his understanding and answers. And

JESUS IN THE MIDST OF THE DOCTORS

when they saw him, they were amazed: and his mother said unto him, "Son, why hast thou thus dealt with us? behold, thy father and I have sought thee sorrowing."

And he said unto them, "How is it that ye sought me? wist ye not that I must be about my Father's business?" And they understood not the saying which he spake unto them.

And he went down with them, and came to Nazareth, and was subject unto them: but his mother kept all these sayings in her heart. Jesus abides in Nazareth And Jesus increased in wisdom and stature, and in favor with God and man.

NOW in the fifteenth year of the reign of Tiberius Cæsar, Pontius Pilate being governor of Judæa, and Herod being tetrarch of Galilee, and his brother Philip tetrarch of Iturea and of the region of Trachonitis, and Lysanias the tetrarch of Abilene, Annas and Caiaphas being the high-priests, the word of God came unto John the Baptist, the son of Zacharias, in the wilderness. And he came into all the country about Jordan, preaching the baptism of repentance for the remission of sins; saying, "Repent ye, for the kingdom of heaven is at hand"; as it is written in the prophets, "Behold, I send my messenger before thy face, which shall prepare thy way before thee." "The voice of one crying in the wilderness, 'Prepare ye the way of the Lord, make his paths straight.' Every valley shall be filled, and every mountain and hill shall be brought low; and the crooked shall be made straight, and the rough ways shall be made smooth; and all flesh shall see the salvation of God."

John the Baptist preaches in the wilderness.

And the same John had his raiment of camel's hair, and a leathern girdle about his loins; and his meat was locusts and wild honey.

Then went out to him Jerusalem, and all Judæa, and all the region round about Jordan, and were baptized of him in Jordon, confessing their sins. But when he saw many of the Pharisees and Sadducees come to his baptism, he said unto them, "O

ORIENTAL MODE OF THRESHING.

generation of vipers, who hath warned you to flee from the wrath to come?

JOHN IN THE WILDERNESS.

bring forth therefore fruits meet for repentance: and think not to say within yourselves, We have Abraham to our father: for I say unto you, that God is able of these stones to raise up children unto Abraham. And now also the ax is laid unto the root of the trees: therefore every tree which bringeth not forth good fruit is hewn down, and cast into the fire."

And the people asked him, saying, "What shall we do then?" He answereth and saith unto them, "He that hath two coats, let him impart to him that hath none; and he that hath meat, let him do likewise." Then came also publicans to be baptized, and said unto him, "Master, what shall we do?" And he said unto them, "Exact no more than that which is appointed you."

He exhorts the people.

And the soldiers likewise demanded of him, saying, "And what shall we do?" And he said unto them, "Do violence to no man, neither accuse any falsely; and be content with your wages."

And as the people were in expectation, and all men mused in their hearts of John, whether he were the Christ, or not: John answered, saying unto them all, "I indeed baptize you with water; but one mightier than I cometh, the latchet of whose shoes I am not worthy to unloose: he shall baptize you with the Holy Ghost and with fire: whose

John prophesies of Christ.

EASTERN METHOD OF WINNOWING GRAIN.

fan is in his hand, and he will thoroughly purge his floor, and will gather the wheat into his garner; but the chaff he will burn with fire unquenchable." And many other things in his exhortation preached he unto the people.

CHAPTER V.

AND Jesus himself began to be about thirty years of age.

Then cometh Jesus from Nazareth of Galilee to Jordan unto John, to be baptized of him. But John forbade him, saying, "I have need to be baptized of thee, and comest thou to me?"

And Jesus answering said unto him, "Suffer it to be so now: for thus it becometh us to fulfill all righteousness." Then he suffered him.

And Jesus, when he was baptized, went up straightway out of the water: and, lo, the heavens were opened unto him, and he saw the Spirit of God *Jesus is baptized of John in the Jordan* descending in a bodily shape like a dove, and lighting upon him: and, lo, a voice from heaven, saying, "This is my beloved Son, in whom I am well pleased."

And Jesus being full of the Holy Ghost returned from Jordan, and was *Jesus is tempted of the Devil* led by the Spirit into the wilderness, being forty days tempted of the Devil; and was with the wild beasts. And in those days he did eat nothing: and when they were ended, he afterward hungered.

And the Devil said unto him, "If thou be the Son of God, command this stone that it be made bread." And Jesus answered him, saying, "It is written, 'That man shall not live by bread alone, but by every word of God.'" And he brought him to Jerusalem, and set him on a pinnacle of the temple, and said unto him, "If thou be the Son of God, cast thyself down from hence: for it is written, 'He shall give his angels charge over thee, to keep thee: and in their hands they shall bear thee up, lest at any time thou dash thy foot against a stone.'" And Jesus answering said unto him, "It is said, 'Thou shalt not tempt the Lord thy God.'" And the Devil, taking him up into an high mountain, showed unto him all the kingdoms of the world in a moment of time. And the Devil said unto him, "All this power will I give thee, and the glory of them: for that is delivered unto me; and to whomsoever I will I give it. If thou therefore wilt worship

THE TEMPTATION.

me, all shall be thine." And Jesus answered and said unto him, "Get thee behind me, Satan: for it is written, 'Thou shalt worship the Lord thy God, and him only shalt thou serve.'"

And when the Devil had ended all the temptation, he departed from him for a season. And, behold, angels came and ministered unto him.

John testifies of Jesus. And this is the record of John, when the Jews sent priests and Levites from Jerusalem to ask him, "Who art thou?" And he confessed, and denied not; but confessed, "I am not the Christ." And they asked him, "What then? Art thou Elias?" And he said, "I am not." "Art thou that prophet?" And he answered, "No." Then said they unto him, "Who art thou? that we may give an answer to them that sent us. What sayest thou of thyself?" He said, "I am the voice of one crying in the wilderness, 'Make straight the way of the Lord,' as said the prophet Esaias."

And they which were sent were of the Pharisees. And they asked him, and said unto him, "Why baptizest thou then, if thou be not that Christ, nor Elias, neither that prophet?"

John answered them, saying, "I baptize with water: but there standeth one among you, whom ye know not; he it is, who coming after me is preferred before me, whose shoe's latchet I am not worthy to unloose."

These things were done in Bethabara beyond Jordan, where John was baptizing.

The next day John seeth Jesus coming unto him, and saith, "Behold the Lamb of God, which taketh away the sin of the world! This is he of whom I said, 'After me cometh a man which is preferred before me; for he was before me.' And I knew him not: but that he should be made manifest to Israel, therefore am I come baptizing with water."

And John bare record, saying, "I saw the Spirit descending from heaven like a dove, and it abode upon him. And I knew him not: but he that sent me to baptize with water, the same said unto me, 'Upon whom thou shalt see the Spirit descending, and remaining on him, the same is he which baptizeth with the Holy Ghost.' And I saw, and bare record that this is the Son of God."

Again, the next day after, John stood, and two of his disciples; and looking upon Jesus as he walked, he saith, "Behold the Lamb of God!" *Two of John's disciples follow Jesus.* And the two disciples heard him speak, and they followed Jesus. Then Jesus turned, and saw them following and saith unto them, "What seek ye?"

They said unto him "Rabbi" (which is to say, being interpreted, Master), "where dwellest thou?"

He saith unto them, "Come and see."

They came and saw where he dwelt, and abode with him that day: for

"BEHOLD THE LAMB OF GOD."

it was about the tenth hour. One of the two which heard John speak, and followed him, was Andrew, Simon Peter's brother. He first findeth his own brother Simon, and saith unto him, "We have found the Messias" (which is, being interpreted, the Christ).

And he brought him to Jesus. And when Jesus beheld him, he said, "Thou art Simon the son of Jona: thou shalt be called Cephas," which is, by interpretation, a stone.

Simon is called Cephas.

The day following Jesus would go forth into Galilee, and findeth Philip, and saith unto him, "Follow me."

Philip and Nathanael are called.

Now Philip was of Bethsaida, the city of Andrew and Peter. Philip findeth Nathanael, and saith unto him, "We have found him, of whom Moses in the law, and the prophets, did write, Jesus of Nazareth, the son of Joseph."

And Nathanael said unto him, "Can there any good thing come out of Nazareth?"

Philip saith unto him, "Come and see."

Jesus saw Nathanael coming to him, and saith of him, "Behold an Israelite indeed, in whom is no guile!"

Nathanael saith unto him, "Whence knowest thou me?"

Jesus answered and said unto him, "Before that Philip called thee, when thou wast under the fig-tree, I saw thee."

Nathanael answered and saith unto him, "Rabbi, thou art the Son of God; thou art the King of Israel."

Jesus answered and said unto him, "Because I said unto thee, I saw thee under the fig-tree, believest thou? thou shalt see greater things than these." And he saith unto him, "Verily, verily, I say unto you, Hereafter ye shall see heaven open, and the angels of God ascending and descending upon the Son of man."

CHAPTER VI.

EARLY MINISTRY.

ND the third day there was a marriage in Cana of Galilee; and the mother of Jesus was there: and both Jesus was called, and his disciples, to the marriage.

And when they wanted wine, the mother of Jesus saith unto him, "They have no wine."

Jesus saith unto her, "Woman, what have I to do with thee? mine hour is not yet come."

His mother saith unto the servants, "Whatsoever he saith unto you, do it."

And there were set there six water-pots of stone, after the manner of the purifying of the Jews, containing two or three firkins apiece. Jesus saith unto them, "Fill the water-pots with water." And they filled them to the brim. And he saith unto them, "Draw out now, and bear unto the governor of the feast." Jesus turns water into wine.

And they bare it. When the ruler of the feast had tasted the water that was made wine, and knew not whence it was (but the servants which drew the water knew), the governor of the feast called the bridegroom, and saith unto him, "Every man at the beginning doth set forth good wine; and when men have well drunk, then that which is worse: but thou hast kept the good wine until now."

This beginning of miracles did Jesus in Cana of Galilee, and manifested forth his glory; and his disciples believed on him.

After this he went down to Capernaum, he, and his mother, and his brethren, and his disciples; and they continued there not many days. And the Jews' passover was at hand, and Jesus went up to Jerusalem, and found in the temple those that sold oxen and sheep and doves, and the changers of money sitting: and when he had made a scourge of small cords, he drove them all out of the temple, and the sheep, and the oxen: and poured out the changers' money, and overthrew the tables; and said unto them that sold doves, "Take these things hence; make not my Father's house a house of merchandise." And Sojourns in Capernaum Cleanses the temple

JESUS DRIVES THE MONEY-CHANGERS FROM THE TEMPLE.

his disciples remembered that it was written, " The zeal of thine house hath eaten me up."

Then answered the Jews and said unto him, "What sign showest thou unto us, seeing that thou doest these things?"

Jesus answered and said unto them, "Destroy this temple, and in three days I will raise it up."

Then said the Jews, "Forty-and-six years was this temple in building, and wilt thou rear it up in three days?"

But he spake of the temple of his body. When therefore he was risen from the dead, his disciples remembered that he had said this unto them: and they believed the scripture, and the word which Jesus had said.

Now when he was in Jerusalem at the passover, in the feast-day, many believed in his name, when they saw the miracles which he did. But Jesus did not commit himself unto them, because he knew all men, and needed not that any should testify of man: for he knew what was in man.

There was a man of the Pharisees, named Nicodemus, a ruler of the Jews: the same came to Jesus by night, and said unto him, " Rabbi, we know that thou art a teacher come from God: for no man can do these miracles that thou doest, except God be with him."

Talks with Nicodemus.

Jesus answered and said unto him, "Verily, verily, I say unto thee, Except a man be born again, he cannot see the kingdom of God."

Nicodemus saith unto him, "How can a man be born when he is old? Can he enter the second time into his mother's womb, and be born?"

Jesus answered, "Verily, verily, I say unto thee, Except a man be born of water and of the Spirit, he cannot enter into the kingdom of God. That which is born of the flesh is flesh: and that which is born of the Spirit is spirit. Marvel not that I said unto thee, Ye must be born again. The wind bloweth where it listeth, and thou hearest the sound thereof, but canst not tell whence it cometh, and whither it goeth: so is every one that is born of the Spirit."

Nicodemus answered and said unto him, " How can these things be?"

Jesus answered and said unto him, " Art thou a master of Israel, and knowest not these things? Verily, verily, I say unto thee, We speak that we do know, and testify that we have seen: and ye receive not our witness. If I have told you earthly things, and ye believe not, how shall ye believe, if I tell you of heavenly things? And no man hath ascended up to heaven, but he that came down from heaven, even the Son of man which is in heaven. And as Moses lifted up the serpent in the wilderness, even so must the Son of man be lifted up: that whosoever believeth in him should not perish, but have eternal life. For God so loved the world, that he gave his only begotten Son, that whosoever believeth in him should not perish, but have everlasting life. For God sent not his Son into the world to

NICODEMUS SEEKS JESUS BY NIGHT.

condemn the world; but that the world through him might be saved. He that believeth on him is not condemned: but he that believeth not is condemned already, because he hath not believed in the name of the only begotten Son of God. And this is the condemnation, that light is come into the world, and men loved darkness rather than light, because their deeds were evil. For every one that doeth evil hateth the light, neither cometh to the light, lest his deeds should be reproved. But he that doeth truth cometh to the light, that his deeds may be made manifest, that they are wrought in God."

After these things came Jesus and his disciples into the land of Judæa; and there he tarried with them, and baptized. And John also was baptizing in Ænon, near to Salim, because there was much water *Returns into Judæa.* there: and they came, and were baptized. For John was not yet cast into prison.

Then there arose a question between some of John's disciples and the Jews about purifying. And they came unto John, and said unto him, "Rabbi, he that was with thee beyond Jordan, to whom thou bearest witness, behold, the same baptizeth, and all men come to him."

John answered and said, "A man can receive nothing, except it be given him from heaven. Ye yourselves bear me witness, that I said, *The answer of John to his disciples* I am not the Christ, but that I am sent before him. He that hath the bride is the bridegroom: but the friend of the bridegroom, which standeth and heareth him, rejoiceth greatly because of the bridegroom's voice: this my joy therefore is fulfilled. He must increase, but I must decrease. He that cometh from above is above all: he that is of the earth is earthly, and speaketh of the earth: he that cometh from heaven is above all. And what he hath seen and heard, that he testifieth; and no man receiveth his testimony. He that hath received his testimony hath set to his seal that God is true. For he whom God hath sent speaketh the words of God: for God giveth not the Spirit by measure unto him. The Father loveth the Son, and hath given all things into his hand. He that believeth on the Son hath everlasting life; and he that believeth not the Son shall not see life; but the wrath of God abideth on him."

CHAPTER VII

IN SAMARIA AND GALILEE.

WHEN therefore the Lord knew how the Pharisees had heard that Jesus made and baptized more disciples than John (though Jesus himself baptized not, but his disciples), he left Judæa, and departed again into Galilee. And he must needs go through Samaria. Then cometh he to a city of Samaria, which is called Sychar, near to the parcel of ground that Jacob gave to his son Joseph. Now Jacob's well was there. Jesus therefore, being wearied with his journey, sat thus on the well: and it was about the sixth hour.

There cometh a woman of Samaria to draw water: Jesus saith unto her,
Jesus talks with a Samaritan woman. "Give me to drink." (For his disciples were gone away unto the city to buy meat.)

Then saith the woman of Samaria unto him, "How is it that thou, being a Jew, askest drink of me, which am a woman of Samaria? for the Jews have no dealings with the Samaritans."

Jesus answered and said unto her, "If thou knewest the gift of God, and who it is that saith to thee, Give me to drink; thou wouldst have asked of him, and he would have given thee living water."

The woman saith unto him, "Sir, thou hast nothing to draw with, and the well is deep: from whence then hast thou that living water? Art thou greater than our father Jacob, which gave us the well, and drank thereof himself, and his children, and his cattle?"

Jesus answered and said unto her, "Whosoever drinketh of this water shall thirst again; but whosoever drinketh of the water that I shall give him shall never thirst; but the water that I shall give him shall be in him a well of water springing up into everlasting life."

The woman saith unto him, "Sir, give me this water, that I thirst not, neither come hither to draw."

Jesus saith unto her, "Go, call thy husband, and come hither."

The woman answered and said, "I have no husband."

Jesus saith unto her, "Thou hast well said, I have no husband: for thou

JESUS TALKS WITH THE SAMARITAN WOMAN.

hast had five husbands; and he whom thou now hast is not thy husband: in that saidst thou truly."

The woman saith unto him, "Sir, I perceive that thou art a prophet. Our fathers worshiped in this mountain; and ye say that in Jerusalem is the place where men ought to worship."

Jesus saith unto her, "Woman, believe me, the hour cometh, when ye shall neither in this mountain nor yet at Jerusalem worship the Father. Ye worship ye know not what: we know what we worship; for salvation is of the Jews. But the hour cometh, and now is, when the true worshipers shall worship the Father in spirit and in truth: for the Father seeketh such to worship him. God is a Spirit: and they that worship him must worship him in spirit and in truth."

The woman saith unto him, "I know that Messias cometh, which is called Christ: when he is come, he will tell us all things."

Jesus saith unto her, "I that speak unto thee am he."

And upon this came his disciples, and marveled that he talked with the woman: yet no man said, "What seekest thou?" or, "Why talkest thou with her?"

The woman then left her water-pot, and went her way into the city, and saith to the men, "Come, see a man which told me all things that ever I did: is not this the Christ?" Then they went out of the city, and came unto him.

In the mean while his disciples prayed him, saying, "Master, eat."

But he said unto them, "I have meat to eat that ye know not of."

Therefore said the disciples one to another, "Hath any man brought him aught to eat?"

Jesus saith unto them, "My meat is to do the will of him that sent me, and to finish his work. Say not ye, There are yet four months, and then cometh harvest? behold, I say unto you, Lift up your eyes, and look on the fields: for they are white already to harvest. And he that reapeth receiveth wages, and gathereth fruit unto life eternal: that both he that soweth and he that reapeth may rejoice together. And herein is that saying true, One soweth, and another reapeth. I sent you to reap that whereon ye bestowed no labor: other men labored, and ye are entered into their labors."

And many of the Samaritans of that city believed on him for the saying
Many Samaritans are converted. of the woman, which testified, He told me all that ever I did. So when the Samaritans were come unto him, they besought him that he would tarry with them: and he abode there two days. And many more believed because of his own word: and said unto the woman, "Now we believe, not because of thy saying: for we have heard him ourselves, and know that this is indeed the Christ, the Saviour of the world."

Now after two days he departed thence, and went into Galilee, preaching the gospel of the kingdom of God, and saying, "The time is fulfilled, and the kingdom of God is at hand: repent ye, and believe the gospel." And there went out a fame of him through all the region round about. For Jesus himself testified, "that a prophet hath no honor in his own country." Then when he was come into Galilee, the Galileans received him, having seen all the things that he did at Jerusalem at the feast: for they also went unto the feast.

Jesus returns to Galilee.

So Jesus came again into Cana of Galilee, where he made the water wine. And there was a certain nobleman, whose son was sick at Capernaum. When he heard that Jesus was come out of Judæa into Galilee, he went unto him, and besought him that he would come down, and heal his son: for he was at the point of death.

He heals a nobleman's son.

Then said Jesus unto him, "Except ye see signs and wonders, ye will not believe."

The nobleman saith unto him, "Sir, come down ere my child die."

Jesus saith unto him, "Go thy way; thy son liveth."

And the man believed the word that Jesus had spoken unto him, and he went his way. And as he was now going down, his servants met him, and told him, saying, "Thy son liveth." Then inquired he of them the hour when he began to amend. And they said unto him, "Yesterday at the seventh hour the fever left him." So the father knew that it was at the same hour in the which Jesus said unto him, Thy son liveth: and himself believed, and his whole house. This is again the second miracle that Jesus did, when he was come out of Judæa into Galilee.

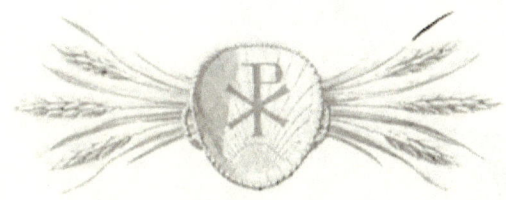

HEALING OF THE IMPOTENT MAN AT THE POOL.

CHAPTER VIII.

THE IMPOTENT MAN HEALED.

AFTER this there was a feast of the Jews; and Jesus went up to Jerusalem.

Now there is at Jerusalem, by the sheep market, a pool, which is called in the Hebrew tongue Bethesda, having five porches. In these lay a great multitude of impotent folk, of blind, halt, withered, waiting for the moving of the water. For an angel went down at a certain season into the pool, and troubled the water: whosoever then first after the troubling of the water stepped in was made whole of whatsoever disease he had. And a certain man was there, which had an infirmity thirty-and-eight years.

Jesus heals an impotent man.

When Jesus saw him lie, and knew that he had been now a long time in that case, he saith unto him, "Wilt thou be made whole?"

The impotent man answered him, "Sir, I have no man, when the water is troubled, to put me into the pool: but while I am coming, another steppeth down before me."

Jesus saith unto him, "Rise, take up thy bed, and walk."

And immediately the man was made whole, and took up his bed, and walked: and on the same day was the Sabbath.

The Jews therefore said unto him that was cured, "It is the Sabbath day: it is not lawful for thee to carry thy bed."

He answered them, "He that made me whole, the same said unto me, 'Take up thy bed, and walk.'"

Then asked they him, "What man is that which said unto thee, Take up thy bed, and walk?"

And he that was healed wist not who it was: for Jesus had conveyed himself away, a multitude being in that place.

Afterward Jesus findeth him in the temple, and said unto him, "Behold, thou art made whole: sin no more, lest a worse thing come unto thee."

The man departed, and told the Jews that it was Jesus which had made him whole. And therefore did the Jews persecute Jesus, and sought to slay him, because he had done these things on the Sabbath day. But Jesus answered them, "My Father worketh hitherto, and I work." Therefore the Jews sought the more to kill him, because he not only had broken the Sabbath, but said also that God was his father, making himself equal with God.

Defends himself for healing on the Sabbath.

Then answered Jesus and said unto them, "Verily, verily, I say unto you, The Son can do nothing of himself, but what he seeth the Father do; for what things soever he doeth, these also doeth the Son likewise. For the Father loveth the Son, and showeth him all things that himself doeth: and he will show him greater works than these, that ye may marvel. For as the Father raiseth up the dead, and quickeneth them; even so the Son quickeneth whom he will. For the Father judgeth no man, but hath committed all judgment unto the Son: that all men should honor the Son, even as they honor the Father. He that honoreth not the Son honoreth not the Father which hath sent him. Verily, verily, I say unto you, He that heareth my word, and believeth on him that sent me, hath everlasting life, and shall not come into condemnation; but is passed from death unto life. Verily, verily, I say unto you, The hour is coming, and now is, when the dead shall hear the voice of the Son of God; and they that hear shall live. For as the Father hath life in himself, so hath he given to the Son to have life in himself; and hath given him authority to execute judgment also, because he is the Son of man. Marvel not at this: for the hour is coming, in the which all that are in the graves shall hear his voice, and shall come forth; they that have done good, unto the resurrection of life; and they that have done evil, unto the resurrection of damnation. I can of mine own self do nothing: as I hear, I judge; and my judgment is just: because I seek not mine own will, but the will of the Father which hath sent me.

Declareth his own dignity.

"If I bear witness of myself, my witness is not true. There is another that beareth witness of me; and I know that the witness which he witnesseth of me is true. Ye sent unto John, and he bare witness unto the truth. But I receive not testimony from man: but these things I say, that ye might be saved. He was a burning and a shining light; and ye were willing for a season to rejoice in his light.

"But I have greater witness than that of John: for the works which the Father hath given me to finish, the same works that I do bear witness of me, that the Father hath sent me. And the Father himself, which hath sent me, hath borne witness of me. Ye have neither heard his voice at any time, nor seen his shape. And ye have not his word abiding in you: for whom he hath sent, him ye believe not. Search the Scriptures; for in them ye think ye have eternal life: and they are they which testify of me. And ye will not come to me, that ye might have life.

JESUS REJECTED AT NAZARETH.

"I receive not honor from men. But I know you, that ye have not the love of God in you. I am come in my Father's name, and ye receive me not: if another shall come in his own name, him ye will receive. How can ye believe, which receive honor one of another, and seek not the honor that cometh from God only?

"Do not think that I will accuse you to the Father: there is one that accuseth you, even Moses, in whom ye trust. For had ye believed Moses, ye would have believed me: for he wrote of me. But if ye believe not his writings, how shall ye believe my words?"

JESUS PREACHES FROM A SHIP.

AND he came to Nazareth, where he had been brought up: and, as his custom was, he went into the synagogue on the Sabbath day, and stood up for to read. And there was delivered unto him the book of the Prophet Isaiah.

And when he had opened the book, he found the place where it was written, "The Spirit of the Lord is upon me, because he hath anointed me to preach the gospel to the poor; he hath

Jesus preaches in the synagogue at Nazareth.

sent me to heal the broken-hearted, to preach deliverance to the captives, and recovering of sight to the blind, to set at liberty them that are bruised, to preach the acceptable year of the Lord."

And he closed the book, and he gave it again to the minister, and sat down. And the eyes of all them that were in the synagogue were fastened on him. And he began to say unto them, "This day is this scripture fulfilled in your ears."

And all bare him witness, and wondered at the gracious words which proceeded out of his mouth. And they said, "Is not this Joseph's son?"

And he said unto them, "Ye will surely say unto me this proverb, Physician, heal thyself: whatsoever we have heard done in Capernaum, do also here in thy country." And he said, "Verily, I say unto you, No prophet is accepted in his own country. But I tell you of a truth, many widows were in Israel in the days of Elijah, when the heaven was shut up three years and six months, when great famine was throughout all the land; but unto none of them was Elijah sent, save unto Zarephath, a city of Zidon, unto a woman that was a widow. And many lepers were in Israel in the time of Elisha the prophet; and none of them was cleansed, saving Naaman the Syrian."

And all they in the synagogue, when they heard these things, were filled

He is rejected by the people of Nazareth.

with wrath, and rose up, and thrust him out of the city, and led him unto the brow of the hill whereon their city was built, that they might cast him down headlong. But he passing through the midst of them went his way.

THE CALLING OF THE FISHERMEN.

And leaving Nazareth, he came and dwelt in Capernaum, which is upon
Takes up his abode in Capernaum. the sea-coast, in the borders of Zebulon and Naphtali: that it
might be fulfilled which was spoken by Isaiah the prophet, say-
ing, "The land of Zebulon, and the land of Naphtali, by the way of the
sea, beyond Jordan, Galilee of the Gentiles; the people which sat in darkness saw a great light; and to them which sat in the region and shadow of
death light is sprung up."

And Jesus, walking by the sea of Galilee, saw two brethren, Simon
called Peter, and Andrew his brother, casting a net into the sea: for
they were fishers. And it came to pass, that, as the people pressed upon
him to hear the word of God, he saw two ships standing by the lake.
And he entered into one of the ships, which was Simon's, and prayed him
that he would thrust out a little from the land. And he sat down, and
taught the people out of the ship.

Now when he had left speaking, he said unto Simon, "Launch out into
A miraculous draught of fishes. the deep, and let
down your nets for
a draught."

FISHING NET.

And Simon answering said unto him, "Master we have toiled
all the night, and have taken
nothing: nevertheless at thy word
I will let down the net." And
when they had this done, they in-
closed a great multitude of fishes:
and their net brake. And they
beckoned unto their partners,
which were in the other ship, that
they should come and help them.

And they came, and filled both the ships, so that they began to sink. When
Simon Peter saw it, he fell down at Jesus' knees, saying, "Depart from me:
for I am a sinful man, O Lord." For he was astonished, and all that were
with him, at the draught of the fishes which they had taken: and so was
also James, and John, and the sons of Zebedee, which were partners with
Simon.

And Jesus said unto them, "Come ye after me, and I will make you to
Peter, James, and John called. become fishers of men." And straightway they forsook their
nets, and followed him. And when he had gone a little farther
thence, he saw James the son of Zebedee, and John his brother, who also
were in the ship mending their nets. And straightway he called them;
and they left their father Zebedee in the ship with the hired servants, and
went after him.

And they went into Capernaum: and straightway on the Sabbath day

he entered into the synagogue, and taught. And they were astonished
at his doctrine: for he taught them as one that had authority,
and not as the scribes.

Heals a demoniac
in Capernaum.

And there was in the synagogue a man with an unclean spirit; and he
cried out, saying, "Let us alone, what have we to do with thee, thou Jesus
of Nazareth? art thou come to destroy us? I know thee who thou art, the
Holy One of God."

And Jesus rebuked him, saying, "Hold thy peace, and come out of him."
And when the unclean spirit had torn him, and cried with a loud voice, he
came out of him. And they were all amazed, insomuch that they questioned
among themselves, saying, "What thing is this? what new doctrine is this?
for with authority commandeth he even the unclean spirits, and they do
obey him." And immediately his fame spread abroad throughout all the
region round about Galilee.

And forthwith, when they were come out of the synagogue, they entered
into the house of Simon with James and John. And when Jesus was
come into Peter's house, he saw his wife's mother laid, and sick
of a fever. And he came and took her by the hand, and
lifted her up; and immediately the fever left her, and she ministered unto
them.

Heals Peter's
wife's mother of a
fever.

And at even, when the sun did set, they brought unto him all that were
diseased, and them that were possessed with devils. And all the city was
gathered together at the door. And he healed many that were
sick of divers diseases, and he cast out the spirits with his
word, and healed all that were sick: that it might be fulfilled which was
spoken by Isaiah the prophet, saying, "Himself took our infirmities, and
bare our sicknesses."

He heals many.

And in the morning, rising up a great while before day, he went out, and
departed into a solitary place, and there prayed. And Simon
and they that were with him followed after him. And when
they had found him, they said unto him, "All men seek for thee."

He retires from
the multitude.

And he said unto them, "Let us go into the next towns, that I may
preach there also: for therefore came I forth."

And Jesus went about all Galilee, teaching in their synagogues, and
preaching the gospel of the kingdom, and healing all manner of sickness
and all manner of disease among the people. And his fame
went throughout all Syria: and they brought unto him all sick
people that were taken with divers diseases and torments, and those which
were possessed with devils, and those which were lunatic, and those that
had the palsy; and he healed them. And there followed him great multitudes of people from Galilee, and from Decapolis, and from Jerusalem, and
from Judea, and from beyond Jordan.

Maketh a cir-
cuit of Galilee.

THE LEPER

And it came to pass, when he was in a certain city, behold a man full of leprosy: who seeing Jesus fell on his face, and besought him, saying, "Lord, if thou wilt, thou canst make me clean."

Healeth a leper.

And Jesus, moved with compassion, put forth his hand, and touched him, saying, "I will: be thou clean."

And as soon as he had spoken, immediately the leprosy departed from him, and he was cleansed. And he straitly charged him, and forthwith sent him away; and said unto him, "See thou say nothing to any man: but go thy way, shew thyself to the priest, and offer for thy cleansing those things which Moses commanded, for a testimony unto them."

But he went out, and began to publish it much, and to blaze abroad the matter, insomuch that Jesus could no more openly enter into the city, but was without in desert places: and great multitudes came together to hear, and to be healed by him of their infirmities.

And again he entered into Capernaum after some days. And it came to pass on a certain day, as he was teaching, that there were Pharisees and doctors of the law sitting by, which were come out of every town of Galilee, and Judæa, and Jerusalem: and straightway many were gathered together, insomuch that there was no room to receive them, no, not so much as about the door: and the power of the Lord was present to heal them. And, behold, men brought in a bed a man which was taken with a palsy: and they sought means to bring him in, and to lay him before him. And when they could not find by what way they

Healeth a paralytic and forgiveth sins.

might bring him in because of the multitude, they went upon the housetop, and let him down through the tiling with his couch into the midst before Jesus. And when he saw their faith, he said unto him, "Son, be of good cheer; thy sins are forgiven thee."

And the scribes and the Pharisees began to reason in their hearts, saying, "Who is this which speaketh blasphemies? who can forgive sins, but God alone?"

But when Jesus perceived their thoughts, he answering said unto them, "What reason ye in your hearts? whether is easier, to say, Thy sins be forgiven thee; or to say, Rise up and walk? but that ye may know that the Son of man hath power upon earth to forgive sins," (he said unto the sick of the palsy,) "I say unto thee, Arise, and take up thy couch, and go unto thine house."

And immediately he rose up before them, and took up that whereon he lay, and departed to his own house, glorifying God. And they were all amazed, and they glorified God, and were filled with fear, saying, "We have seen strange things to-day. We never saw it on this fashion."

JESUS HEALS THE MAN WITH THE PALSY.

67

CHAPTER X.

CALLING OF THE TWELVE, AND OTHER INCIDENTS.

ND he went forth again by the seaside; and all the multitude resorted unto him, and he taught them. And as he passed by, he saw Levi the son of Alphæus sitting at the receipt of custom, and said unto him, "Follow me." And he left all, rose up, and followed him. And Levi made him a great feast in his own house. And it came to pass, as Jesus sat at meat in the house, behold, many publicans and

Matthew is called, and maketh a feast for Jesus.

sinners came and sat down with him and his disciples. And when the Pharisees saw it, they said unto his disciples, "Why eateth your Master with publicans and sinners?" But when Jesus heard that, he said unto them, "They that be whole need not a physician, but they that are sick. But go ye and learn what that meaneth, I will have mercy, and not sacrifice: for I am not come to call the righteous, but sinners to repentance."

Then came to him the disciples of John, saying, "Why do we and the Pharisees fast oft and make prayers, but thy disciples fast not?"

And Jesus said unto them, "Can the children of the bridechamber fast, while the bridegroom is with them? as long as they have the bridegroom with them, they cannot fast. But the

GOAT-SKIN BOTTLES.

days will come, when the bridegroom shall be taken away from them, and then shall they fast in those days."

And he spake also a parable unto them: "No man putteth a piece of a new garment upon an old; if otherwise, then both the new maketh a rent,

and the piece that was taken out of the new agreeth not with the old. And no man putteth new wine into old bottles; else the new wine will burst the bottles, and be spilled, and the bottles shall perish. But new wine must be put into new bottles; and both are preserved. No man also having drunk old wine straightway desireth new: for he saith, The old is better."

And it came to pass on the second sabbath after the first, that he went The Pharisees complain of the disciples for plucking corn on the sabbath. through the corn-fields; and his disciples plucked the ears of corn, and did eat, rubbing them in their hands. And certain of the Pharisees said unto them, "Why do ye that which is not lawful to do on the sabbath days?"

And Jesus answering them said, "Have ye not read so much as this, what David did, when himself was an hungered, and they which were with him; how he went into the house of God in the days of Abiather the high-priest, and did eat the shewbread, which was not lawful for him to eat, neither for them which were with him, but only for the priests? or have ye not read in the law, how that on the sabbath days the priests in the temple profane the sabbath, and are blameless? but I say unto you, That in this place is one greater than the temple. But if ye had known what this meaneth, I will have mercy, and not sacrifice, ye would not have condemned the guiltless. The sabbath was made for man, and not man for the sabbath: therefore the Son of man is Lord also of the sabbath."

And when he was departed thence, he went into their synagogue: and there was a man whose right hand was withered. And the scribes and A man with a withered hand healed on the sabbath. Pharisees watched him, whether he would heal on the sabbath day: that they might find an accusation against him. But he knew their thoughts, and said unto the man which had the withered hand, "Rise up, and stand forth in the midst."

And he arose and stood forth. And they asked him, saying, "Is it lawful to heal on the sabbath days?"

Then said Jesus unto them, "I will ask you one thing; Is it lawful on the sabbath days to do good, or to do evil? to save life, or to destroy it?" And he said unto them, "What man shall there be among you, that shall have one sheep, and if it fall into a pit on the sabbath day, will he not lay hold on it, and lift it out? how much then is a man better than a sheep?"

But they held their peace. And when he had looked round about on them with anger, being grieved for the hardness of their hearts, he saith unto the man, "Stretch forth thy hand."

And he stretched it out: and his hand was restored whole as the other. The Pharisees and Herodians conspire against him. And the Pharisees filled with madness went forth, and straightway took counsel with the Herodians against him, how they might destroy him. But Jesus withdrew himself with his disci-

ples to the sea: and a great multitude from Galilee followed him, and
from Judæa, and from Jerusalem, and from Idumæa, and from beyond
Jordan; and they about Tyre and Sidon, a great multitude, when they
heard what great things he did, came unto him. And he spake to his
Many miracles wrought. disciples, that a small ship should wait on him because of the
multitude, lest they should throng him. For he had healed
many; insomuch that they pressed upon him for to touch him, as many
as had plagues. And unclean spirits, when they saw him, fell down before
him, and cried, saying, "Thou art the Son of God." And he straitly
charged them that they should not make him known.

That it might be fulfilled which was spoken by Isaiah the prophet,
saying, "Behold my servant, whom I have chosen; my beloved, in whom
A prophecy fulfilled. my soul is well pleased: I will put my
spirit upon him, and he shall shew judg-
ment to the Gentiles. He shall not strive, nor cry;
neither shall any man hear his voice in the streets.
A bruised reed shall he not break, and smoking flax
shall he not quench, till he send forth judgment unto
victory. And in his name shall the Gentiles trust."

LANTERN LAMP WITH FLAXEN WICK.

And it came to pass in those days, that he went
out into a mountain to pray, and continued all night
in prayer to God. And when it was day, he calleth
The twelve Apostles set apart. unto him whom he would: and they came unto him. And
he ordained twelve, that they should be with him, and that
he might send them forth to preach, and to have power to heal sicknesses, and to cast out devils, whom also he named apostles: Simon,
(whom he also named Peter,) and Andrew his brother, James the son of
Zebedee, and John the brother of James; and he surnamed them Boan-
erges, which is "The sons of Thunder": Philip and Bartholomew, Matthew the publican, and Thomas, James the son of Alphæus, and Simon
the Canaanite called Zelotes, and Judas the brother of James, and Judas
Iscariot, which also was the traitor.

And he came down with them, and stood in the plain, and the company
of his disciples, and a great multitude of people out of all Judæa and
Jerusalem, and from the sea-coast of Tyre and Sidon, which came to hear
him, and to be healed of their diseases: and they that were vexed with
unclean spirits: and they were healed. And the whole multitude sought
to touch him: for there went virtue out of him, and healed them all.

CHAPTER XI.

THE SERMON ON THE MOUNT.

AND seeing the multitudes, he went up into a mountain; and when he was set, his disciples came unto him: and he opened his mouth, and taught them, saying, "Blessed are the poor in spirit: for theirs is the kingdom of heaven. Blessed are they that mourn: for they shall be comforted. Blessed are the meek: for they shall inherit the earth. Blessed are they which do hunger and thirst after righteousness: for they shall be filled. Blessed are the merciful: for they shall obtain mercy. Blessed are the pure in heart: for they shall see God. Blessed are the peacemakers: for they shall be called the children of God. Blessed are they which are persecuted for righteousness' sake: for theirs is the kingdom of heaven. Blessed are ye, when men shall revile you, and persecute you, and shall say all manner of evil against you falsely, for my sake. Rejoice ye in that day, and leap for joy: for, behold, your reward is great in heaven: for in the like manner did their fathers unto the prophets.

The Beatitudes.

"But woe unto you that are rich! for ye have received your consolation. Woe unto you that are full! for ye shall hunger. Woe unto you that laugh now! for ye shall mourn and weep. Woe unto you, when all men shall speak well of you! for so did their fathers to the false prophets.

"Ye are the salt of the earth: but if the salt have lost his savor, wherewith shall it be salted? it is thenceforth good for nothing, but to be cast out, and to be trodden under foot of men.

The salt of the earth.

Ye are the light of the world. A city that is set on an hill cannot be hid. Neither do men light a candle, and put it under a bushel, but on a candlestick; and it giveth light unto all that are in the

The light of the world.

EASTERN CANDLESTICK WITH LAMP.

JOSEPH IN PRAYER.

house. Let your light so shine before men, that they may see your good works, and glorify your Father which is in heaven.

"Think not that I am come to destroy the law, or the prophets: I am not come to destroy, but to fulfill. For verily I say unto you, Till heaven and earth pass, one jot or one tittle shall in no wise pass from the law, till all be fulfilled. Whosoever therefore shall break one of these least commandments, and shall teach men so, he shall be called the least in the kingdom of heaven: but whosoever shall do and teach them, the same shall be called great in the kingdom of heaven. For I say unto you, That except your righteousness shall exceed the righteousness of the Scribes and Pharisees, ye shall in no case enter into the kingdom of heaven.

Of keeping the commandments.

"Ye have heard that it was said by them of old time, Thou shalt not kill; and whosoever shall kill shall be in danger of the judgment: but I say unto you, That whosoever is angry with his brother without a cause shall be in danger of the judgment; and whosoever shall say to his brother, Raca, shall be in danger of the council: but whosoever shall say, Thou fool, shall be in danger of hell-fire. Therefore if thou bring thy gift to the altar, and there rememberest that thy brother hath aught against thee; leave there thy gift before the altar, and go thy way; first be reconciled to thy brother, and then come and offer thy gift. Agree with thine adversary quickly, while thou art in the way with him; lest at any time the adversary deliver thee to the judge, and the judge deliver thee to the officer, and thou be cast into prison. Verily I say unto thee, Thou shalt by no means come out thence, till thou hast paid the uttermost farthing.

Of anger.

"Ye have heard that it was said by them of old time, Thou shalt not commit adultery; but I say unto you, That whosoever looketh on a woman to lust after her hath committed adultery with her already in his heart. And if thy right eye offend thee, pluck it out, and cast it from thee: for it is profitable for thee that one of thy members should perish, and not that thy whole body should be cast into hell. And if thy right hand offend thee, cut it off, and cast it from thee: for it is profitable for thee that one of thy members should perish, and not that thy whole body should be cast into hell. It hath been said, Whosoever shall put away his wife, let him give her a writing of divorcement: but I say unto you, That whosoever shall put away his wife, saving for the cause of fornication, causeth her to commit adultery: and whosoever shall marry her that is divorced committeth adultery.

Of impurity.

"Again, ye have heard that it hath been said by them of old time, Thou shalt not forswear thyself, but shalt perform unto the Lord thine oaths: but I say unto you, Swear not at all; neither by

Of swearing.

heaven; for it is God's throne: nor by the earth; for it is his footstool:
neither by Jerusalem; for it is the city of the great King. Neither shalt
thou swear by thy head, because thou canst not make one hair white or
black. But let your communication be, Yea, yea; Nay, nay: for whatsoever is more than these cometh of evil.

"Ye have heard that it hath been said, An eye for an eye, and a tooth
for a tooth: but I say unto you, That ye resist not evil: but whosoever shall
smite thee on thy right cheek, turn to him the other also. And
Of revenge. if any man will sue thee at the law, and take away thy coat,
let him have thy cloak also. And whosoever shall compel thee to go a mile,
go with him twain. Give to him that asketh thee, and from him that
would borrow of thee turn not thou away.

"Ye have heard that it hath been said, Thou shalt love thy neighbor,
Of love to ene- and hate thine enemy. But I say unto you, Love your enemies,
mies. bless them that curse you, do good to them that hate you, and
pray for them which despitefully use you, and persecute you; that ye may
be the children of your Father which is in heaven: for he maketh his sun
to rise on the evil and on the good, and sendeth rain on the just and on the
unjust. For if ye love them which love you, what thank have ye? for
sinners also love those that love them. And if ye do good to them which
do good to you, what thank have ye? for sinners also do even the same.
And if ye lend to them of whom ye hope to receive, what thank have ye?
for sinners also lend to sinners, to receive as much again. But love ye your
enemies, and do good, and lend, hoping for nothing again; and your
reward shall be great, and ye shall be the
children of the Highest: for he is kind
unto the unthankful and to the evil. Be
ye therefore perfect even as your Father
which is in heaven is perfect.

"Take heed that ye do not your alms
before men, to be seen of them: otherwise
Of alms. ye have no reward of your
Father which is in heaven.
Therefore when thou doest thine alms,
do not sound a trumpet before thee, as
the hypocrites do in the synagogues and
in the streets, that they may have glory
of men. Verily I say unto you, They
have their reward. But when thou doest
alms, let not thy left hand know what
thy right hand doeth: that thine alms

ORIENTAL PRAYING IN THE STREET.

may be in secret: and thy Father which seeth in secret himself shall reward
thee openly.

THE PRAYER IN SECRET.

"And when thou prayest, thou shalt not be as the hypocrites are: for they love to pray standing in the synagogues and in the corners of the streets, that they may be seen of men. Verily I say unto you,

Of prayer.

They have their reward. But thou, when thou prayest, enter into thy closet, and when thou hast shut thy door, pray to thy Father which is in secret; and thy Father which seeth in secret shall reward thee openly. But when ye pray, use not vain repetitions, as the heathen do: for they think that they shall be heard for their much speaking. Be not ye therefore like unto them: for your Father knoweth what things ye have need of, before ye ask him.

"After this manner therefore pray ye: Our Father which art in heaven,

The Lord's Prayer.

Hallowed be thy name. Thy kingdom come. Thy will be done in earth, as it is in heaven. Give us this day our daily bread. And forgive us our debts, as we forgive our debtors. And lead us not into temptation, but deliver us from evil: For thine is the kingdom, and the power, and the glory, forever. Amen.

"For if ye forgive men their trespasses, your heavenly Father will also

Of forgiveness.

forgive you: but if ye forgive not men their trespasses, neither will your Father forgive your trespasses.

"Moreover when ye fast, be not, as the hypocrites, of a sad countenance:

Of fasting.

for they disfigure their faces, that they may appear unto men to fast. Verily I say unto you, They have their reward. But thou, when thou fastest, anoint thine head, and wash thy face; that thou appear not unto men to fast, but unto thy Father which is in secret: and thy Father, which seeth in secret, shall reward thee openly.

"Lay not up for yourselves treasures upon earth, where moth and rust

Of treasure in heaven.

doth corrupt, and where thieves break through and steal: but lay up for yourselves treasures in heaven, where neither moth nor rust doth corrupt, and where thieves do not break through nor steal: for where your treasure is, there will your heart be also.

"The light of the body is the eye; if therefore thine eye be single, thy

Of a single eye.

whole body shall be full of light. But if thine eye be evil, thy whole body shall be full of darkness. If therefore the light that is in thee be darkness, how great is that darkness!

"No man can serve two masters: for either he will hate the one, and love the other; or else he will hold to the one and despise the other. Ye cannot serve God and mammon. Therefore I say unto you, Take no thought for

Of carefulness about this life.

your life, what ye shall eat, or what ye shall drink; nor yet for your body, what ye shall put on. Is not the life more than meat, and the body than raiment? Behold the fowls of the air; for they sow not, neither do they reap, nor gather into barns: yet your heavenly Father feedeth them. Are ye not much better than they? which of you by taking thought can add one cubit unto his stature? and why take ye thought for raiment? Consider the lilies of the field, how they grow; they toil not, neither do they spin; and yet I say unto you, That even Solomon in all his glory was not arrayed like one of these. Wherefore, if God so clothe the grass of the field, which to-day is, and to-morrow is cast into the

FLOWERS OF THE FIELD GATHERED IN GALILEE.

oven, shall he not much more clothe you, O ye of little faith? therefore take no thought, saying, What shall we eat? or, What shall we drink? or, Wherewithal shall we be clothed? (for after all these things do the Gentiles seek :) for your heavenly Father knoweth that ye have need of these things. But seek ye first the kingdom of God, and his righteousness; and all these things shall be added unto you. Take therefore no thought for the morrow; for the morrow shall take thought for the things of itself. Sufficient unto the day is the evil thereof.

"Judge not, and ye shall not be judged: condemn not, and ye shall not
Of uncharitable judgments.　be condemned: forgive, and ye shall be forgiven: give, and it shall be given unto you: good measure, pressed down, and shaken together, and running over, shall men give into your bosom. For with the same measure that ye mete withal it shall be measured to you again."

And he spake a parable to them, "Can the blind lead the blind? shall they not both fall into the ditch? the disciple is not above his master: but every one that is perfect shall be as his master. And why beholdest thou the mote that is in thy brother's eye, and considerest not the beam that is in thine own eye? or how wilt thou say to thy brother, Let me pull out the mote out of thine eye; and, behold, a beam is in thine own eye? thou hypocrite, first cast out the beam out of thine own eye; and then shalt thou see clearly to cast out the mote out of thy brother's eye.

BUYING CORN WITH FLY-GLASS.

"Give not that which is holy unto the dogs, neither cast ye your pearls
Of casting pearls before swine.　before swine, lest they trample them under their feet, and turn again and rend you.

"Ask, and it shall be given you; seek, and ye shall find; knock, and it
Of asking and receiving.　shall be opened unto you: for every one that asketh receiveth; and he that seeketh findeth; and to him that knocketh it shall be opened. Or what man is there of you, whom if his son ask bread, will he give him a stone? or if he ask a fish, will he give him a serpent? if ye then, being evil, know how to give good gifts unto your children, how much more shall your Father which is in heaven give good things to them that ask him? therefore all things whatsoever ye would that men should do to you, do ye even so to them: for this is the law and the prophets.

"Enter ye in at the strait gate: for wide is the gate, and broad is the
Of the strait gate.　way, that leadeth to destruction, and many there be which go in thereat: because strait is the gate, and narrow is the way, which leadeth unto life, and few there be that find it.

"Beware of false prophets, which come to you in sheep's clothing, but inwardly they are ravening wolves. Ye shall know them by their fruits. Do men gather grapes of thorns, or figs of thistles? even so every good tree bringeth forth good fruit: but a corrupt tree bringeth forth evil fruit. A good tree cannot bring forth evil fruit, neither can a corrupt tree bring forth good fruit. Every tree that bringeth not forth good fruit is hewn down, and cast into the fire. Wherefore by their fruits ye shall know them. A good man out of the good treasure of his heart bringeth forth that which is good; and an evil man out of the evil treasure of his heart bringeth forth that which is evil: for of the abundance of the heart his mouth speaketh. *Of false prophets.*

"Not every one that saith unto me, Lord, Lord, shall enter into the kingdom of heaven: but he that doeth the will of my Father which is in heaven. Many will say to me in that day, Lord, Lord, have we not prophesied in thy name? and in thy name have cast out devils? and in thy name done many wonderful works? and then will I profess unto them, I never knew you: depart from me, ye that work iniquity. *Not profession but deeds the test of men.*

"Therefore whosoever heareth these sayings of mine, and doeth them, I will liken him unto a wise man, which built his house upon a rock: and the rain descended, and the floods came, and the winds blew, and beat upon that house; and it fell not: for it was founded upon a rock. And every one that heareth these sayings of mine, and doeth them not, shall be likened unto a foolish man, which built his house upon the sand: and the rain descended, and the floods came, and the winds blew, and beat upon that house; and it fell: and great was the fall of it." *Of hearing and doing.*

And it came to pass, when Jesus had ended these sayings, the people were astonished at his doctrine: for he taught them as one having authority, and not as the scribes. When he was come down from the mountain, great multitudes followed him.

CHAPTER XII.

OW when he had ended all his sayings in the audience of the people, he entered into Capernaum. And a certain centurion's servant, who was dear unto him, was sick, and ready to die. And when he heard of Jesus, he sent unto him the elders of the Jews, beseeching him that he would come and heal his servant. And when they came to Jesus, they besought him instantly, saying, That he was worthy for whom he should do this: for he loveth our nation, and he hath built us a synagogue. Then Jesus went with them.

And when he was now not far from the house, the centurion sent friends to him, saying unto him, "Lord, trouble not thyself: for I am not worthy that thou shouldest enter under my roof: wherefore neither thought I myself worthy to come unto thee: but say in a word, and my servant shall be healed. For I also am a man set under authority, having under me soldiers, and I say unto one, Go, and he goeth; and to another, Come, and he cometh; and to my servant, Do this, and he doeth it.

A centurion's servant healed.

When Jesus heard these things, he marveled at him, and turned him about, and said unto the people that followed him, "I say unto you, I have not found so great faith, no, not in Israel. Many shall come from the east and west, and shall sit down with Abraham, and Isaac, and Jacob, in the kingdom of heaven. But the children of the kingdom shall be cast out into outer darkness: there shall be weeping and gnashing of teeth." And they that were sent, returning to the house, found the servant whole that had been sick.

And it came to pass the day after, that he went into a city called Nain; and many of his disciples went with him, and much people. Now when he came nigh to the gate of the city, behold, there was a dead man carried out, the only son of his mother, and she was a widow: and much people of the city was with her. And when the Lord saw her, he had compassion on her, and said unto her, "Weep not."

HEALING THE CENTURION'S SERVANT

And he came and touched the bier; and they that bare him stood still.
And he said, "Young man, I say unto thee, Arise." And he that was dead
sat up, and began to speak. And he delivered him to his
mother. And there came a fear on all; and they glorified
God, saying, "That a great prophet is risen up among us"; and, "That
God hath visited his people." And this rumor of him went forth throughout all Judæa, and throughout all the region round about.

A widow's son raised from the dead.

And the disciples of John showed him of all these things. And John
calling unto him two of his disciples sent them to Jesus, saying,
"Art thou he that should come? or look we for another?"

The message of John the Baptist.

When the men were come unto him, they said, "John Baptist hath sent
us unto thee, saying, Art thou he that should come? or look we for another?"

And in the same hour he cured many of their infirmities and plagues, and
of evil spirits; and unto many that were blind he gave sight. Then Jesus
answering said unto them, "Go your way, and tell John what things ye
have seen and heard: how that the blind see, the lame walk, the lepers are
cleansed, the deaf hear, the dead are raised, to the poor the gospel is
preached. And blessed is he, whosoever shall not be offended in me."

And when the messengers of John
were departed, he began to speak
unto the people concerning John,
"What went ye out into
the wilderness for to see?
A reed shaken with the wind? but
what went ye out for to see? A
man clothed in soft raiment? Behold, they which are gorgeously ap-
pareled, and live delicately, are in
kings' courts. But what went ye
out for to see? A prophet? Yea, I
say unto you, and much more than
a prophet. For this is he, of whom
it is written, Behold, I send my
messenger before thy face, which
shall prepare thy way before thee.
Verily I say unto you, Among them
that are born of women there hath
not risen a greater than John the
Baptist: notwithstanding he that is

Christ's testimony to John.

PAPYRUS REEDS ON THE UPPER JORDAN.

least in the kingdom of heaven is greater than he. And from the days of
John the Baptist until now the kingdom of heaven suffereth violence, and

THE SON OF THE WIDOW OF NAIN.

THE BURNING OF SODUS MILL

7

the violent take it by force. For all the prophets and the law prophesied until John. And if ye will receive it, this is Elias, which was for to come. He that hath ears to hear, let him hear."

And all the people that heard him, and the publicans, justified God, being baptized with the baptism of John. But the Pharisees and lawyers rejected the counsel of God against themselves, being not baptized of him.

And the Lord said, "Whereunto then shall I liken the men of this generation? and to what are they like? they are like unto children sitting in the market-place, and calling one to another, and say- *John and Christ* ing, 'We have piped unto you, and ye have not danced; we have mourned to you, and ye have not wept.' For John the Baptist came neither eating bread nor drinking wine; and ye say, 'He hath a devil.' The Son of man is come eating and drinking; and ye say, 'Behold a gluttonous man, and a wine-bibber, a friend of publicans and sinners!' But wisdom is justified of all her children."

Then began he to upbraid the cities wherein most of his mighty works were done, because they repented not: "Woe unto thee, Chorazin! *He upbraids* woe unto thee, Bethsaida! for if the mighty works, which were *certain cities* done in you, had been done in Tyre and Sidon, they would have repented long ago in sackcloth and ashes. But I say unto you, It shall be more tolerable for Tyre and Sidon in the day of judgment than for you. And thou, Capernaum, which art exalted unto heaven, shalt be brought down to hell: for if the mighty works, which have been done in thee, had been done in Sodom, it would have remained until this day. But I say unto you, That it shall be more tolerable for the land of Sodom in the day of judgment, than for thee."

At that time Jesus answered and said, "I thank thee, O Father, Lord of heaven and earth, because thou hast hid these things from the wise and prudent, and hast revealed them unto babes. Even so, Father: for so it seemed good in thy sight.

"All things are delivered unto me of my Father: and no man knoweth the Son but the Father; neither knoweth any man the Father, save the Son, and he to whomsoever the Son will reveal him.

"Come unto me, all ye that labor and are heavy laden, and I will give you rest. Take my yoke upon you, and learn of me; for I am *A gracious invi-* meek and lowly of heart; and ye shall find rest unto your souls. *tation* For my yoke is easy and my burden is light."

And one of the Pharisees desired him that he would eat with him. And he went into the Pharisee's house, and sat down to meat. And *Washes the* behold, a woman in the city, which was a sinner, when she knew *Lord's feet with tears.* that Jesus sat at meat in the Pharisee's house, brought an alabaster box of ointment, and stood at his feet behind him weeping, and began to wash

his feet with tears, and did wipe them **with the** hairs of her head, and kissed his feet, and anointed them with the ointment. Now **when the** Pharisee which had bidden him saw it, he spake within himself, saying, " This man, if he were a prophet, would have known who and what manner of woman this is that toucheth him : for she is a sinner."

And Jesus answering said **unto** him, " Simon, I have somewhat **to say** unto thee."

And he saith, " Master, say **on.**"

" There was a certain creditor which had two debtors : **the one owed five** hundred pence, and the other fifty. And when they had noth-ing to pay, he frankly forgave them both. Tell me therefore, which of them will love him most ?" Simon **answered and** said, " I sup-**pose** that he, to whom he forgave most."

The two debtors.

And he said unto him, " Thou hast rightly judged."

And he turned to the woman, and said unto Simon, " **Seest** thou this woman ? I entered into thine house, thou gavest me no water for my feet : but she hath washed my feet with tears, and wiped them with the hairs of her head. Thou gavest me no kiss : but this woman since the time I came in hath not ceased to kiss my feet. My head with oil thou didst not anoint : but this woman hath **anointed** my feet with ointment. Wherefore I **say** unto thee, Her sins, which **are** many, are forgiven ; for **she loved much :** but to whom little is forgiven, the same loveth little."

And he said unto her, " Thy sins are forgiven."

And they that sat at meat with him began to say within **themselves, Who** is this that forgiveth sins also ?

And he said to the woman, " Thy **faith** hath saved **thee :** go in peace."

And Jesus went about all the cities and villages, teaching **in** their syna-gogues, and preaching the gospel of the kingdom, and healing every sick-ness and every disease among the people. And **the twelve** were with him, and certain women, which had been healed of evil spirits and infirmities, Mary called Magdalene, out of whom went seven devils, and Joanna the wife of Chuza, Herod's steward, and Susanna, **and** many others, which ministered unto him of their substance.

Then was brought unto him one possessed with a devil, blind, and dumb : and he healed him, insomuch that the blind and dumb both spake and saw. And all the people were amazed, and said, " Is not this the son of David ?"

A deaf and dumb demoniac healed.

But when the Pharisees heard it, they **said,** " This fellow doth not cast out devils, but by Beelzebub **the prince of the** devils."

The Pharisees blaspheme.

And Jesus knew their **thoughts, and said** unto them, " **Every kingdom divided** against itself **is brought to desolation : and every** city or house divided against itself shall not stand: and if Satan cast out Satan, he is divided against himself; how shall then his kingdom stand? And if I by Beelzebub cast out devils, by whom do your children cast them out? therefore they shall be your judges. But if I cast out devils by the Spirit of God, then the kingdom of God is come unto you. Or else how can one enter into a strong man's house, and spoil his goods, except he first bind the strong man? and then he will spoil his house. He that is not with me is against me; and he that gathereth not with me scattereth abroad.

"Wherefore I say unto you, All manner of sin and blasphemy shall be forgiven unto men: but the blasphemy against the Holy Ghost shall not be forgiven unto men. And whosoever speaketh a word against the Son of man, it shall be forgiven him: but whosoever speaketh against the Holy Ghost, it shall not be forgiven him, neither in this world, neither in the world to come: because they said, He hath an unclean spirit.

"Either make the tree good, and his fruit good; or else make the tree corrupt, and his fruit corrupt: for the tree is known by his fruit. O generation of vipers, how can ye, being evil, speak good things? for out of the abundance of the heart the mouth speaketh. A good man out of the good treasure of the heart bringeth forth good things: and an evil man out of the evil treasure bringeth forth evil things. But I say unto you, That every idle word that men shall speak, they shall give account thereof in the day of judgment. For by thy words thou shalt be justified, and by thy words thou shalt be condemned."

JESUS TEACHING IN THE SYNAGOGUE.

CHAPTER XIII.

SEASIDE PARABLES.

HE same day went Jesus out of the house, and sat by the seaside. And he began again to teach by the seaside: and there was gathered unto him a great multitude, so that he entered into a ship, and sat in the sea; and the whole multitude was by the sea on the land.

And he taught them many things by parables, and said unto them in his doctrine, "Hearken; Behold, there went out a sower to sow: and it came to pass, as he sowed, some fell by the wayside; and it was trodden down, and the fowls of the air devoured it. And some fell on stony ground, where it had not much earth; and immediately it sprang up, because it had no depth of earth: but when the sun was up, it was scorched; and because it had no root, it withered away. And some fell among thorns, and the thorns grew up, and choked it, and it yielded no fruit. And other fell on good ground, and did yield fruit that sprang up and increased: and brought forth, some thirty, and some sixty, and some an hundred."

The sower.

And when he had said these things, he cried, "He that hath ears to hear, let him hear."

And when he was alone, they that were about him with the twelve asked of him the parable, saying, "What might this parable be? and why speakest thou unto them in parables?"

And he said unto them, "Unto you it is given to know the mystery of the kingdom of God: but unto them that are without, all these things are done in parables. For whosoever hath, to him shall be given, and he shall have more abundance: but whosoever hath not, from him shall be taken away even that he hath. Therefore speak I to them in parables, that seeing they may see, and not perceive: and hearing they may hear, and not understand; lest at any time they should be converted, and their sins should be forgiven them. And in them is fulfilled the prophecy of Isaiah, which saith, By hearing ye shall hear, and shall not understand; and seeing ye shall see, and shall not perceive: for this

Why Jesus taught in parables.

people's heart is waxed gross, and their ears are dull of hearing, and their eyes they have closed; lest at any time they should see with their eyes, and hear with their ears, and should understand with their heart, and should be converted, and I should heal them. But blessed are your eyes, for they see: and your ears, for they hear. For verily I say unto you, That many prophets and righteous men have desired to see those things which ye see, and have not seen them; and to hear those things which ye hear, and have not heard them."

And he said unto them, "Know ye not this parable? and how then will ye know all parables? Hear ye therefore the parable of the sower. The interpretations of the parable of the sower. The sower soweth the word. When any one heareth the word of the kingdom, and understandeth it not, then cometh the wicked one, and catcheth away that which was sown in his heart. This is he which received seed by the wayside. But he that received the seed

EASTERN PLOUING AND SOWING.

into stony places, the same is he that heareth the word, and anon with joy receiveth it; yet hath he not root in himself, but dureth for a while: for when tribulation or persecution ariseth because of the word, by and by he is offended. He also that received seed among the thorns is he that heareth the word; and the cares of this world, and the deceitfulness of riches, and the lusts of other things entering in, choke the word, and it becometh unfruitful. But he that received seed into good ground is he that heareth the word, and receiveth it in an honest and good heart and understandeth it: which also beareth fruit, with patience, and bringeth forth, some an hundred fold, some sixty, some thirty.

"No man, when he hath lighted a candle, covereth it with a vessel, or putteth it under a bed; but setteth it on a candlestick, that they which All hidden things shall be published. enter in may see the light. For nothing is secret, that shall not be made manifest; neither anything hid, that shall not be known and come abroad. Take heed therefore how ye hear: for whosoever hath, to him shall be given; and whosoever hath not, from him shall be taken even that which he seemeth to have."

Another parable put he forth unto them, saying, "The kingdom of heaven is likened unto a man which sowed good seed in his field: but while men slept his enemy came and sowed tares among the wheat, and *The tares in the field.* went his way. But when the blade was sprung up, and brought forth fruit, then appeared the tares also. So the servants of the householder came and said unto him, "Sir, didst not thou sow good seed in thy field? from whence then hath it tares?" He said unto them, "An enemy hath done this." The servants said unto him, "Wilt thou then that we go and gather them up?" But he said, "Nay; lest while ye gather up the tares, ye root up also the wheat with them. Let both grow together until the harvest: and in the time of harvest I will say to the reapers, Gather ye together first the tares, and bind them in bundles to burn them: but gather the wheat into my barn."

And he said, "So is the kingdom of God, as if a man should cast seed into the ground; and should sleep, and rise night and day, and the seed should spring and grow up, he knoweth *The seed growing secretly.* not how. For the earth bringeth forth fruit of herself; first the blade, then the ear, after that the full corn in the ear. But when the fruit is brought forth, immediately he putteth in the sickle, because the harvest is come."

SYRIAN AND EGYPTIAN WHEAT.

Another parable put he forth unto them, saying, "The kingdom of heaven is like to a grain of mustard-seed, which a man took, and *The grain of mustard seed.* sowed in his field: which indeed is the least of all seeds: but when it is grown, it is the greatest among herbs, and becometh a tree, so that the birds of the air come and lodge in the branches thereof."

Another parable spake he unto them: "The kingdom of heaven is like unto leaven, *The leaven hid in the meal.* which a woman took, and hid in three measures of meal, till the whole was leavened."

All these things spake Jesus unto the multitude in parables; as they were able to hear it. But without a parable spake he not unto them: and when they were alone, he expounded all things to his disciples: that it might be fulfilled which was spoken by the prophet, saying, "I will open my mouth in parables; I will utter things which have been kept secret from the foundation of the world."

Then Jesus sent the multitude away, and went into the house: and his disciples came unto him, saying, "Declare unto us the parable of the tares of the field." He answered and said unto them, "He that soweth the good seed is the Son of man; the field is the world; the good seed are the children of the kingdom; but the tares are the children of the wicked one;

The interpreta-tion of the para-ble of the tares. the enemy that sowed them is the devil; the harvest is the end of the world; and the reapers are the angels. As therefore the tares are gathered and burned in the fire; so shall it be in the end of this world. The Son of man shall send forth his angels, and they shall gather out of his kingdom all things that offend, and them which do iniquity; and shall cast them into a furnace of fire: there shall be wailing and gnashing of teeth. Then shall the righteous shine forth as the sun in the kingdom of their Father. Who hath ears to hear, let him hear.

"Again, the kingdom of heaven is like unto treasure hid in a field; the

The treasure hid in a field. which when a man hath found, he hideth, and for joy thereof goeth and selleth all that he hath, and buyeth that field.

"Again, the kingdom of heaven is like unto a merchantman, seeking

The pearl of great price. goodly pearls: who, when he had found one pearl of great price, went and sold all that he had, and bought it.

"Again, the kingdom of heaven is like unto a net, that was cast into the sea, and gathered of every kind: which, when it was full, they drew to

The net cast into the sea. shore, and sat down, and gathered the good into vessels, but cast the bad away. So shall it be at the end of the world: the angels shall come forth, and sever the wicked from among the just, and shall cast them into the furnace of fire: there shall be wailing and gnashing of teeth."

Jesus saith unto them, "Have ye understood all these things?"

They say unto him, Yea, Lord.

Then said he unto them, "Therefore every scribe which is instructed

The instructed teacher. unto the kingdom of heaven is like unto a man that is an householder, which bringeth forth out of his treasure things new and old."

And it came to pass, that when Jesus had finished these parables, he departed thence.

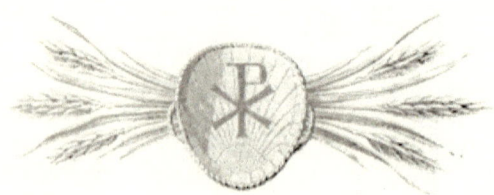

OW when Jesus saw great multitudes about him, he gave commandment to depart unto the other side. And when he was entered into a ship, his disciples followed him, and they launched forth. And, behold, there arose a great tempest in the sea, insomuch that the ship was covered with the waves. And he was in the hinder part of the ship, asleep on a pillow : and they awake him, and say unto him, "Master, carest thou not that we perish ?" And he arose, and rebuked the wind, and said unto the sea, "Peace, be still."

And the wind ceased, and there was a great calm. And he said unto them, "Why are ye so fearful ? how is it that ye have no faith ?" And they feared exceedingly, and said one to another, "What manner of man is this, that even the wind and the sea obey him ?"

And they came over unto the other side of the sea, into the country of the Gadarenes, which is over against Galilee. And when he was come out of the ship, immediately there met him out of the tombs a man, which had devils long time, and ware no clothes, who had his dwelling among the tombs; and no man could bind him, no, not with chains: because that he had been often bound with fetters and chains, and the chains had been plucked asunder by him, and the fetters broken in pieces: neither could any man tame him. And always, night and day, he was in the mountains, and in the tombs, crying, and cutting himself with stones. But when he saw Jesus afar off, he ran and worshiped him, and cried with a loud voice, and said, "What have I to do with thee, Jesus, thou Son of the most high God ? I adjure thee by God, that thou torment me not." For he said unto him, "Come out of the man, thou unclean spirit." And he asked him, "What is thy name ?" And he answered, saying, "My name is Legion: for we are many." And he besought him much that he would not send them away out of the country, into the deep.

Now there was there nigh unto the mountains a great herd of swine feeding. And all the devils besought him, saying, "Send us into the swine,

that we may enter into them." And forthwith Jesus gave them leave. And the unclean spirits went out, and entered into the swine: and the herd ran violently down a steep place into the sea, (they were about two thousand;) and were choked in the sea. And they that fed the swine fled, and told it in the city, and in the country. And they went out to see what it was that was done; and came to Jesus, and found the man out of whom the devils were departed, sitting at the feet of Jesus, clothed and in his right mind: and they were afraid. And they that saw it told them how it befell to him that was possessed with the devil, and also concerning the swine. Then the whole multitude of the country of the Gadarenes round about besought him to depart from them; for they were taken with great fear: and he went up into the ship, and returned back again. Now the man out of whom the devils were departed besought him that he might be with him. Howbeit Jesus suffered him not, but saith unto him, "Go home to thy friends, and tell them how great things the Lord hath done for thee, and hath had compassion on thee." And he departed, and began to publish in Decapolis how great things Jesus had done for him: and all men did marvel.

And he entered into a ship, and passed over, and came into his own city. And much people gathered unto him, for they were all waiting for him.

A WOMAN HEALED BY TOUCHING THE GARMENT OF JESUS.

CHAPTER XV.

ND behold, there cometh one of the rulers of the synagogue, Jairus by name; and when he saw him, he fell at his feet, and besought him greatly, saying, "My little daughter lieth at the point of death," (for he had one only daughter:) "I pray thee, come and lay thy hands on her, that she may be healed; and she shall live."

And Jesus arose, and followed him, and so did his disciples, and much people followed him, and thronged him. And a certain woman, which had an issue of blood twelve years, and had suffered many things of many physicians, and had spent all that she had, and was nothing bettered, but rather grew worse, when she had heard of Jesus, came in the press behind, and touched his garment. For she said, "If I may touch but his clothes, I shall be whole." And straightway the fountain of her blood was dried up: and she felt in her body that she was healed of that plague. And Jesus said, "Who touched me?" When all denied, Peter and they that were with him said, "Master, the multitude throng thee and press thee, and sayest thou, 'Who touched me?'" And Jesus said, "Somebody hath touched me: for I perceive that virtue is gone out of me."

And when the woman saw that she was not hid, she came trembling, and falling down before him, she declared unto him before all the people for what cause she had touched him, and how she was healed immediately. And he said unto her, "Daughter, be of good comfort: thy faith hath made thee whole; go in peace, and be whole of thy plague."

While he yet spake, there came from the ruler of the synagogue's house certain which said, "Thy daughter is dead: why troublest thou the Master any further?" As soon as Jesus heard the word that was spoken, he saith unto the ruler of the synagogue, "Be not afraid, only believe, and she shall be made whole." And he suffered no man to follow him, save Peter, and James, and John the brother of James. And he cometh to the house of the ruler of the synagogue, and seeth the tumult, and them that wept and wailed greatly. And when he

The ruler's daughter having died, is raised from the dead.

THE DAUGHTER OF JAIRUS RAISED FROM THE DEAD

was come in, he saith unto them, "Why make ye this ado, and weep?" And they laughed him to scorn, knowing that she was dead. But when he had put them all out, he taketh the father and the mother of the damsel, and them that were with him, and entered in where the damsel was lying. And he took the damsel by the hand, and said unto her, "Talitha cumi"; (which is, being interpreted, "Damsel, I say unto thee, arise.")

And straightway the damsel arose, and walked; for she was of the age of twelve years. And they were astonished with a great astonishment. And he charged them straitly that no man should know it; and commanded that something should be given her to eat. And the fame hereof went abroad into all that land.

And when Jesus departed thence, two blind men followed him, crying, and saying, "Thou son of David, have mercy on us." And when he was come into the house, the blind men came to him: and Jesus saith unto them, "Believe ye that I am able to do this?" They said unto him, "Yea, Lord." Then touched he their eyes, saying, "According to your faith be it unto you." And their eyes were opened; and Jesus straitly charged them, saying, "See that no man know it." But they, when they were departed, spread abroad his fame in all that country.

Two blind men are healed.

As they went out, behold, they brought to him a dumb man possessed with a devil. And when the devil was cast out, the dumb spake: and the multitudes marveled, saying, "It was never so seen in Israel." But the Pharisees said, "He casteth out devils through the prince of the devils."

A dumb demoniac healed.

And he went out from thence, and came into his own country; and his disciples follow him. And when the sabbath day was come, he began to teach in the synagogue: and many hearing him were astonished, saying, "Whence hath this man this wisdom, and these mighty works? Is not this the carpenter's son? is not his mother called Mary? and his brethren, James, and Joses, and Simon, and Judas? and his sisters, are they not all with us? Whence then hath this man all these things?" And they were offended in him. But Jesus said unto them, "A prophet is not without honor, but in his own country, and among his own kin, and in his own house." And he could there do no mighty work, save that he laid his hands upon a few sick folk, and healed them. And he marveled because of their unbelief.

He teacheth in Nazareth.

But when he saw the multitudes, he was moved with compassion on them, because they fainted, and were scattered abroad, as sheep having no shepherd. Then saith he unto his disciples, "The harvest truly is plenteous, but the laborers are few; pray ye therefore the Lord of the harvest, that he will send forth laborers into his harvest."

He pitieth the multitude.

And when he had called unto him his twelve disciples, he gave them

HEALING OF TWO BLIND MEN.

power against unclean spirits, to cast them out, and to heal all manner of sickness and all manner of disease. And he began to send them forth by two and two: and commanded them, saying, "Go not into the way of the Gentiles, and into any city of the Samaritans enter ye not: but go rather to the lost sheep of the house of Israel. And as ye go, preach, saying, The kingdom of heaven is at hand. Heal the sick, cleanse the lepers, raise the dead, cast out devils: freely ye have received, freely give. Provide neither gold, nor silver, nor brass in your purses, nor scrip for your journey, nor yet staves, neither two coats, neither shoes, but be shod with sandals: for the workman is worthy of his meat. And into whatsoever city or town ye shall enter, inquire who in it is worthy; and there abide till ye go thence. And when ye come into an house, salute it. And if the house be worthy, let your peace come upon it: but if it be not worthy, let your peace return to you. And whosoever shall not receive you, nor hear your words, when ye depart out of that house or city, shake off the dust of your feet, for a testimony against them. Verily I say unto you, It shall be more tolerable for the land of Sodom and Gomorrah in the day of judgment, than for that city.

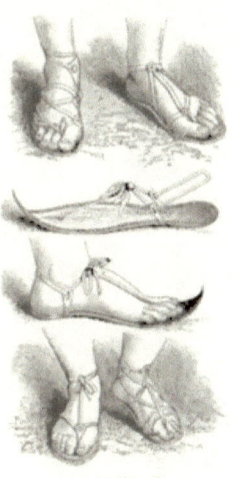

SANDALS.

"Behold, I send you forth as sheep in the midst of wolves; be ye therefore wise as serpents, and harmless as doves. But beware of men; for they will deliver you up to the councils, and they will scourge you in their synagogues; and ye shall be brought before governors and kings for my sake, for a testimony against them and the Gentiles. But when they deliver you up, take no thought how or what ye shall speak: for it shall be given you in that same hour what ye shall speak. For it is not ye that speak, but the Spirit of your Father which speaketh in you. And the brother shall deliver up the brother to death, and the father the child: and the children shall rise up against their parents, and cause them to be put to death. And ye shall be hated of all men for my name's sake: but he that endureth to the end shall be saved. But when they persecute you in this city, flee ye into another: for verily I say unto you, Ye shall not have gone over the cities of Israel, till the Son of man be come. The disciple is not above his master, nor the servant above his lord. It is enough for the disciple that he be as his master, and the servant as his lord. If they have called the master of the house Beelzebub, how much more shall they call them of his household?

BEHEADING OF JOHN THE BAPTIST.

" Fear them not therefore: for there is nothing covered, that shall not be revealed; and hid, that shall not be known. What I tell you in darkness, that speak ye in light: and what ye hear in the ear, that preach ye upon the house-tops. And fear not them which kill the body, but are not able to kill the soul; but rather fear him which is able to destroy both soul and body in hell. Are not two sparrows sold for a farthing? and one of them shall not fall on the ground without your Father. But the very hairs of your head are all numbered. Fear ye not, therefore, ye are of more value than many sparrows. Whosoever therefore shall confess me before men, him will I confess also before my Father which is in heaven. But whosoever shall deny me before men, him will I also deny before my Father which is in heaven.

" Think not that I am come to send peace on earth: I came not to send peace, but a sword. For I am come to set a man at variance against his father, and the daughter against her mother, and the daughter-in-law against her mother-in-law. And a man's foes shall be they of his own household. He that loveth father or mother more than me is not worthy of me; and he that loveth son or daughter more than me is not worthy of me. And he that taketh not his cross, and followeth after me, is not worthy of me. He that findeth his life shall lose it: and he that loseth his life for my sake shall find it.

" He that receiveth you receiveth me, and he that receiveth me receiveth him that sent me. He that receiveth a prophet in the name of a prophet shall receive a prophet's reward; and he that receiveth a righteous man in the name of a righteous man shall receive a righteous man's reward. And whosoever shall give to drink unto one of these little ones a cup of cold water only in the name of a disciple, verily I say unto you, he shall in no wise lose his reward."

And they went out and preached that men should repent. And they cast out many devils, and anointed with oil many that were sick, and healed them everywhere. *The preaching of the twelve.*

And it came to pass, that when Jesus had made an end of commanding his twelve disciples, he departed thence to teach and to preach in their cities. *The departure of Jesus from Nazareth.*

And king Herod heard of him; (for his name was spread abroad;) and he said, That John the Baptist was risen from the dead, and therefore mighty works do show forth themselves in him. *Herod hears of Christ.* Others said, " That it is Elias." And others said, " That it is a prophet, or as one of the prophets." But when Herod heard thereof, he said, " It is John, whom I beheaded: he is risen from the dead."

For Herod himself had sent forth and laid hold upon John, and bound him in prison for Herodias's sake, his brother Philip's wife: for he had

married her. For John had said unto Herod, "It is not lawful for thee
to have thy brother's wife." Therefore Herodias had a quarrel
against him, and would have killed him; but she could not:
For Herod feared John, knowing that he was a just man and a holy, and
observed him; and when he heard him, he did many things, and heard him
gladly.

The imprison-
ment of John.

And when a convenient day was come, that Herod on his birthday made
a supper to his lords, high captains, and chief estates of Galilee; and
when the daughter of the said Herodias came in, and danced, and pleased
Herod and them that sat with him, the king said unto the damsel, "Ask of
me whatsoever thou wilt, and I give it thee." And he sware unto her,
"Whatsoever thou shalt ask of me, I will give it thee, unto the half of my
kingdom." And she went forth, and said unto her mother, "What shall I
ask?" And she said, "The head of John the Baptist." And she came in
straightway with haste unto the king, and asked, saying, I will that thou
give me by and by in a charger the head of John the Baptist.

And the king was exceeding sorry; yet for his oath's sake, and for
their sakes which sat with him, he would not reject her. And immediately
the king sent an executioner, and commanded his head to be
brought: and he went and beheaded him in the prison. And
brought his head in a charger, and gave it to the damsel: and the damsel
gave it to her mother.

The death of John
the Baptist.

And when his disciples heard of it, they came and took up his corpse,
and laid it in the tomb.

And the apostles, when they were returned, gathered themselves together
unto Jesus, and told him all things, both what they had done,
and what they had taught. And he said unto them, "Come
ye yourselves apart into a desert place, and rest awhile": for there were
many coming and going, and they had no leisure so much as to eat.

The apostles re-
turn unto Jesus.

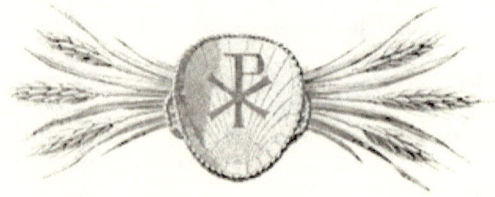

DAUGHTER OF HERODIAS AND THE HEAD OF JOHN THE BAPTIST

CHAPTER XVI.

THE FEEDING OF THE FIVE THOUSAND.

ND Jesus went over the sea of Galilee, which is the sea of Tiberias, into a desert place belonging to the city called Bethsaida. And a great multitude followed him, because they saw his miracles which he did on them that were diseased. And Jesus went up into a mountain, and there he sat with his disciples. And the passover, a feast of the Jews, was nigh. When Jesus then lifted up his eyes, and saw a great company come unto him, he was moved with compassion toward them,

Jesus retires to Bethsaida to rest, and is followed by the multitudes. because they were as sheep not having a shepherd: and he began to teach them many things, and healed them that had need of healing.

And when the day was now far spent, he saith unto Philip, "Whence shall we buy bread, that these may eat?" And this he said to prove him: for he himself knew what he would do. Philip answered him, "Two hundred pennyworth of bread is not sufficient for them, that every one of them may take a little." One of his disciples, Andrew, Simon Peter's brother, saith unto him, "There is a lad here, which hath five barley loaves, and

He feedeth five thousand. two small fishes: but what are they among so many?" And Jesus said, "Make them sit down by fifties in a company." Now there was much grass in the place. So the men sat down, in number about five thousand.

Then he took the five loaves and the two fishes, and looking up to heaven, he blessed them, and brake, and gave to the disciples to set before the multitude. And they did eat, and were all filled. When they were filled, he said unto his disciples, "Gather up the fragments that remain, that nothing be lost." Therefore they gathered them together, and filled twelve baskets with the fragments of the five barley loaves, which remained over and above unto them that had eaten. Then those men, when they had seen the miracle that Jesus did, said, "This is of a truth that prophet that should come into the world."

When Jesus therefore perceived that they would come and take him by

THE MIRACLE OF THE LOAVES 109

force, to make him a king, he departed again into a mountain himself alone. And when even was now come, his disciples went down unto the sea, and entered into a ship, and went over the sea toward Capernaum.   And it was now dark, and Jesus was not come to them.   But the ship was now in the midst of the sea, tossed with waves: for the wind was contrary.   And he saw them toiling in rowing, for the wind was contrary unto them.   And in
Christ walked on the sea. the fourth watch of the night Jesus went unto them, walking on the sea.   And when the disciples saw him walking on the sea, they were troubled, saying, " It is a spirit"; and they cried out for fear. But straightway Jesus spake unto them, saying, " Be of good cheer; it is I ; be not afraid."   And Peter answered him and said, " Lord, if it be thou, bid me come unto thee on the water."   And he said, " Come."

And when Peter was come down out of the ship, he walked on the water, to go to Jesus.   But when he saw the wind boisterous, he was afraid; and beginning to sink, he cried, saying, " Lord, save me."   And immediately Jesus stretched forth his hand, and caught him, and said unto him, " O thou of little faith, wherefore didst thou doubt ?"

And when they were come into the ship, the wind ceased, and immediately the ship was at the land whither they went.   Then they that were in the ship came and worshiped him, saying, " Of a truth thou art the Son of God."

And when they had passed over, they came into the land of Gennesaret, and drew out to the shore.   And when they were come out of the ship, straightway they knew him, and ran through that whole region round
He healeth many in the land of Gennesaret. about, and began to carry about in beds those that were sick, where they heard he was.   And whithersoever he entered, into villages, or cities, or country, they laid the sick in the streets, and besought him that they might touch if it were but the border of his garment: and as many as touched him were made whole.

The day following, when the people which stood on the other side of the sea saw that there was none other boat there, save that one whereinto his disciples were entered, and that Jesus went not with his disciples into the boat, but that his disciples were gone away alone ; (howbeit there came other boats from Tiberias nigh unto the place where they did eat bread, after that the Lord had given thanks :) when the people therefore saw that Jesus was not there, neither his disciples, they also took shipping, and came to Capernaum, seeking for Jesus.   And when they had found him on the other side of the sea, they said unto him, "Rabbi, when camest thou hither ?"   Jesus answered them and said, " Verily, verily, I say unto you, ye seek me, not because ye saw the miracles, but because ye did eat of the loaves, and were filled.   Labor not for the meat which perisheth, but for that meat which endureth unto everlasting life, which the Son of man shall

give unto you: for him hath God the Father sealed." Then said they unto him, " What shall we do, that we might work the works of God ?" Jesus answered and said unto them, " This is the work of God, that ye believe on him whom he hath sent."

They said therefore unto him, " What sign shewest thou then, that we may see, and believe thee ? what dost thou work ? Our fathers did eat manna in the desert ; as it is written, He gave them bread from heaven to eat." Then said Jesus unto them, " Verily, verily, I say unto you, Moses gave you not that bread from heaven ; but my Father giveth you the true bread from heaven. For the bread of God is he which cometh down from heaven, and giveth life unto the world." Then said they unto him, " Lord, evermore give us this bread." And Jesus said unto them, " I am the bread of life : he that cometh to me shall never hunger ; and he that believeth on me shall never thirst. But I said unto you, That ye also have seen me, and believe not. All that the Father giveth me shall come to me ; and him that cometh to me I will in no wise cast out. For I came down from heaven, not to do mine own will, but the will of him that sent me. And this is the Father's will which hath sent me, that of all which he hath given me I should lose nothing, but should raise it up again at the last day. And this is the will of him that sent me, that every one which seeth the Son, and believeth on him, may have everlasting life : and I will raise him up at the last day."

The Jews then murmured at him, because he said, I am the bread which came down from heaven. And they said, " Is not this Jesus, the son of Joseph, whose father and mother we know ? how is it then that he saith, I came down from heaven ?" Jesus therefore answered and said unto them, " Murmur not among yourselves. No man can come to me, except the Father which hath sent me draw him : and I will raise him up at the last day. It is written in the prophets, And they shall be all taught of God. Every man therefore that hath heard, and hath learned of the Father, cometh unto me. Not that any man hath seen the Father, save he which is of God, he hath seen the Father. Verily, verily, I say unto you, He that believeth on me hath everlasting life. I am that bread of life. Your fathers did eat manna in the wilderness, and are dead. This is the bread which cometh down from heaven, that a man may eat thereof and not die. I am the living bread which came down from heaven : if any man eat of this bread, he shall live forever : and the bread that I will give is my flesh, which I will give for the life of the world."

The Jews therefore strove among themselves, saying, " How can this man give us his flesh to eat ?" Then Jesus said unto them, Verily, verily, I say unto you, Except ye eat the flesh of the Son of man, and drink his blood, ye have no life in you. Whoso eateth my flesh, and drinketh my

The bread from heaven.

blood, hath eternal life; and I will raise him up at the last day. For my flesh is meat indeed, and my blood is drink indeed. He that eateth my flesh, and drinketh my blood, dwelleth in me, and I in him. As the living Father hath sent me, and I live by the Father: so he that eateth me, even he shall live by me. This is that bread which came down from heaven: not as your fathers did eat manna, and are dead: he that eateth of this bread shall live forever." These things said he in the synagogue, as he taught in Capernaum.

Many therefore of his disciples, when they had heard of this, said, "This is an hard saying: who can hear it?" When Jesus knew in himself that his disciples murmured at it, he said unto them, "Doth this offend you? What and if ye shall see the Son of man ascend up where he was before? it is the spirit that quickeneth; the flesh profiteth nothing: the words that I speak unto you, they are spirit, and they are life. But there are some of you that believe not." For Jesus knew from the beginning who they were that believed not, and who should betray him. And he said, "Therefore said I unto you, that no man can come unto me, except it were given unto him of my Father."

From that time many of his disciples went back, and walked no more with him. Then said Jesus unto the twelve, "Will ye also go away?" Then Simon Peter answered him, "Lord, to whom shall we go? thou hast the words of eternal life. And we believe and are sure that thou art that Christ, the Son of the living God." Jesus answered them, "Have not I chosen you twelve, and one of you is a devil?" He spake of Judas Iscariot the son of Simon: for he it was that should betray him, being one of the twelve.

After these things Jesus walked in Galilee: for he would not walk in Jewry, because the Jews sought to kill him.

CHAPTER XVII.

THE TRADITION OF THE ELDERS. — THE SYROPHENICIAN WOMAN AND OTHER INCIDENTS.

THEN came together unto him the Pharisees, and certain of the scribes, which came from Jerusalem. And when they saw some of his disciples eat bread with defiled, that is to say, with unwashen, hands, they found fault. For the Pharisees, and all the Jews, except they wash their hands oft, eat not, holding the tradition of the elders. And when they come from the market, except they wash, they eat not. And many other things there be, which they have received to hold, as the washing of cups, and pots, and brazen vessels, and of tables. Then the Pharisees and scribes asked him, "Why walk not thy disciples according to the tradition of the elders, but eat bread with unwashen hands?"

The Pharisees from Jerusalem find fault.

He answered and said unto them, "Well hath Isaiah prophesied of you hypocrites, as it is written, 'This people honoreth me with their lips, but their heart is far from me. Howbeit in vain do they worship me, teaching for doctrines the commandments of men.' For laying aside the commandment of God, ye hold the tradition of men, as the washing of pots and cups: and many other such like things ye do." And he said unto them, "Full well ye reject the commandment of God, that ye may keep your own tradition. For Moses said, 'Honor thy father and thy mother'; and, 'Whoso curseth father or mother, let him die the death': but ye say, 'If a man shall say to his father or mother, It is Corban, that is to say, a gift, by whatsoever thou mightest be profited by me'; he shall be free. And ye suffer him no more to do aught for his father or his mother: making the word of God of none effect through your tradition, which ye have delivered: and many such like things do ye."

He rebuketh them concerning their traditions.

And when he had called all the people unto him, he said unto them, "Hearken unto me every one of you, and understand: There is nothing from without a man, that entering into him can defile him: but the things which come out of him, those are they that defile the

Out of the heart proceed evil thoughts.

man. If any man have ears to hear, let him hear." And when he was entered into the house from the people, his disciples said unto him, "Knowest thou that the Pharisees were offended, after they heard this saying?" But he answered and said, "Every plant, which my heavenly Father hath not planted, shall be rooted up. Let them alone : they be blind leaders of the blind. And if the blind lead the blind, both shall fall into the ditch." Then answered Peter and said unto him, "Declare unto us this parable." And Jesus said, "Are ye also yet without understanding? Do ye not perceive, that whatsoever thing from without entereth into the man, it cannot defile him ; because it entereth not into his heart, but into the belly, and goeth out into the draught, purging all meats?" And he said, "That which cometh out of the man, that defileth the man. For from within, out of the heart of men, proceed evil thoughts, adulteries, fornications, murders, thefts, covetousness, wickedness, deceit, lasciviousness, an evil eye, blasphemy, pride, foolishness : all these evil things come from within, and defile the man : but to eat with unwashen hands defileth not a man."

And from thence he arose, and went into the borders of Tyre and Sidon, *The demoniac daughter of a Syrophenician woman is healed.* and entered into an house, and would have no man know it : but he could not be hid. For a certain woman, whose young daughter had an unclean spirit, heard of him, and came and fell at his feet : the woman was a Greek, a Syrophenician by nation ; and she besought him that he would cast forth the devil out of her daughter. But he answered her not a word. And his disciples came and besought him, saying, Send her away ; for she crieth after us. But he answered and said, "Let the children first be filled : for it is not meet to take the children's bread, and to cast it unto the dogs." And she said, "Truth, Lord : yet the dogs eat of the crumbs which fall from their master's table." Then Jesus answered and said unto her, "O woman, great is thy faith : be it unto thee even as thou wilt." And her daughter was made whole from that very hour.

And again, departing from the coasts of Tyre and Sidon, he came unto the sea of Galilee, through the midst of the coasts of Decapolis. And they bring unto him one that was deaf, and had an impediment in his speech ; and they beseech him to put his hand upon him. And he took him aside from the multitude, and put his fingers into his ears, and he spit, and *He healeth a deaf man.* touched his tongue ; and looking up to heaven, he sighed, and saith unto him, "Ephphatha," (that is, "Be opened.") And straightway his ears were opened, and the string of his tongue was loosed, and he spake plain. And he charged them that they should tell no man : but the more he charged them, so much the more a great deal they published it ; and were beyond measure astonished, saying, He hath done all things well : he maketh both the deaf to hear, and the dumb to speak.

THE SYROPHENICIAN WOMAN.

JESUS HEALS A DEAF MAN.

In those days the multitude being very great, and having nothing to eat, Jesus called his disciples unto him, and saith unto them, "I have compassion on the multitude, because they continue with me now three days, and have nothing to eat: and I will not send them away fasting, lest they faint in the way: for divers of them came from far." And his disciples say unto him, "Whence should we have so much bread in the wilderness, as to fill so great a multitude?" And Jesus saith unto them, "How many loaves have ye?" And they said, "Seven, and a few little fishes." And he commanded the multitude to sit down on the ground. And he took the seven loaves and the fishes, and gave thanks, and brake them, and gave to his disciples, and the disciples to the multitude. And they did all eat, and were filled: and they took up of the broken meat that was left Four thousand seven baskets full. And they that did eat were four thousand people fed. men, beside women and children. And he sent away the multitude, and took ship, and came into the coasts of Magdala and Dalmanutha.

JESUS LEADS THE BLIND.

THE Pharisees also with the Sadducees came, and tempting desired him that he would shew them a sign from heaven. He answered and said unto them, "When it is evening, ye say, It will be fair weather: for the sky is red. And in the morning, It will be foul weather to-day: for the sky is red and lowering. O ye hypocrites, ye can discern the face of the sky; but can ye not discern the signs of the times? A wicked and adulterous generation seeketh after a sign; and there shall no sign be given unto it, but the sign of the prophet Jonas."

And he left them, and departed. And when his disciples were come to the other side, they had forgotten to take bread, neither had they in the ship with them more than one loaf. Then Jesus said unto them, "Take heed and beware of the leaven of the Pharisees and of the Sadducees." And they reasoned among themselves, saying, "It is because we have no bread." And when Jesus knew it, he saith unto them, "Why reason ye, because ye have no bread? perceive ye not yet, neither understand? have ye your heart yet hardened? having eyes, see ye not? and having ears, hear ye not? and do ye not remember? when I brake the five loaves among five thousand, how many baskets full of fragments took ye up?" They say unto him, "Twelve." "And when the seven among four thousand, how many baskets full of fragments took ye up?" And they said, "Seven." And he said unto them, "How is it that ye do not understand that I spake it not to you concerning bread, that ye should beware of the leaven of the Pharisees and of the Sadducees?" Then understood they how that he bade them not beware of the leaven of bread, but of the doctrine of the Pharisees and of the Sadducees.

And he cometh to Bethsaida: and they bring a blind man unto him, and besought him to touch him. And he took the blind man by the hand, and led him out of the town; and when he had spit on his eyes, and put his hands upon him, he asked him if he saw aught. And he looked up, and

JESUS AND HIS DISCIPLES ON THE ROAD TO CÆSAREA.

126

said, "I see men as trees, walking." After that he put his hands again upon his eyes, and made him look up: and he was restored, and saw every man clearly. And he sent him away to his house, saying, "Neither go into the town, nor tell it to any in the town."

He heals a blind man.

When Jesus came into the coasts of Cæsarea Philippi, he asked his disciples, saying, "Whom do men say that I the Son of man am?" And they said, "Some say that thou art John the Baptist; some, Elijah; and others, Jeremiah, or one of the prophets." He saith unto them, "But whom say ye that I am?" And Simon Peter answered and said, "Thou art the Christ, the Son of the living God."

Peter professeth faith.

And Jesus answered and said unto him, "Blessed art thou, Simon Barjona: for flesh and blood hath not revealed it unto thee, but my Father which is in heaven. And I say also unto thee, That thou art Peter, and upon this rock I will build my church; and the gates of hell shall not prevail against it. And I will give unto thee the keys of the kingdom of heaven: and whatsoever thou shalt bind on earth shall be bound in heaven: and whatsoever thou shalt loose on earth shall be loosed in heaven." Then charged he his disciples that they should tell no man that he was Jesus the Christ.

Christ's reply.

From that time forth began Jesus to show unto his disciples, how that "the Son of man must suffer many things, and be rejected of the elders and chief priests and scribes, and be slain, and be raised the third day." And he spake that saying openly. Then Peter took him, and began to rebuke him, saying, "Be it far from thee, Lord: this shall not be unto thee." But he turned, and said unto Peter, "Get thee behind me, Satan: thou art an offence unto me: for thou savorest not the things that be of God, but those that be of men."

Jesus foretelleth his death and reproves Peter.

And when he had called the people unto him with his disciples also, he said unto them, "Whosoever will come after me, let him deny himself, and take up his cross daily, and follow me. For whosoever will save his life shall lose it; but whosoever shall lose his life for my sake and the gospel's, the same shall save it. For what shall it profit a man, if he shall gain the whole world, and lose his own soul? or what shall a man give in exchange for his soul? Whosoever therefore shall be ashamed of me and of my words in this adulterous and sinful generation, of him also shall the Son of man be ashamed, when he cometh in the glory of his Father with the holy angels."

Of bearing the cross.

And he said unto them, "Verily I say unto you, That there be some of them that stand here, which shall not taste of death, till they have seen the kingdom of God come with power."

CHAPTER XIX.

THE TRANSFIGURATION AND CONNECTING INCIDENTS.

ND it came to pass about an eight days after these sayings, he took Peter and John and James, and went up into a high mountain to pray: and was transfigured before them: and his face did shine as the sun, and his raiment was white as the light. And, behold, there talked with him two men, which were Moses and Elijah: who appeared in glory, and spake of his decease which he should accomplish at Jerusalem. But Peter and they that were with him were heavy with sleep: and when they were awake, they saw his glory, and the two men that stood with him.

And it came to pass, as they departed from him, Peter said unto Jesus, "Master, it is good for us to be here: and let us make three tabernacles; one for thee, and one for Moses, and one for Elijah." For he wist not what to say: for they were sore afraid. While he yet spake, behold, a bright cloud overshadowed them: and behold a voice out of the cloud, which said, "This is my beloved Son, in whom I am well pleased; hear ye him." And when the disciples heard it, they fell on their face, and were sore afraid. And Jesus came and touched them, and said, "Arise, and be not afraid." And when they had lifted up their eyes, they saw no man, save Jesus only. And as they came down from the mountain, Jesus charged them, saying, "Tell the vision to no man, until the Son of man be risen again from the dead." And they kept that saying with themselves, questioning one with another what the rising from the dead should mean.

And his disciples asked him, saying, "Why then say the scribes that Elijah must first come?" And Jesus answered and said unto them, "Elijah truly shall first come, and restore all things. But I say unto you, That Elijah is come already, and they knew him not, but have done unto him whatsoever they listed. Likewise shall also the Son of man suffer of them." Then the disciples understood that he spake unto them of John the Baptist.

And when he came to his disciples on the next day, he saw a great multi-

THE TRANSFIGURATION

tude about them, and the scribes questioning with them. And straightway all the people, when they beheld him, were greatly amazed, and running to
He healeth a demoniac child. him saluted him. And he asked the scribes, "What question ye with them?" And there came to him a certain man, kneeling down to him, and saying, "Lord, have mercy on my son: (for he is mine only child:) for he is lunatic, and sore vexed: for ofttimes he falleth into the fire, and oft into the water." And, lo, a spirit taketh him and teareth him: and he foameth, and gnasheth with his teeth, and pineth away: and I spake to thy disciples that they should cast him out: and they could not." He answereth him, and saith, "O faithless generation, how long shall I be with you? how long shall I suffer you? bring him unto me." And they brought him unto him; and when he saw him, straightway the spirit tare him; and he fell on the ground, and wallowed foaming. And he asked his father, "How long is it ago since this came unto him?" And he said, "Of a child. And ofttimes it hath cast him into the fire, and into the waters, to destroy him: but if thou canst do anything, have compassion on us, and help us." Jesus saith unto him, "If thou canst believe, all things are possible to him that believeth." And straightway the father of the child cried out, and said with tears, "Lord, I believe: help thou mine unbelief."

When Jesus saw that the people came running together, he rebuked the foul spirit, saying unto him, "Thou dumb and deaf spirit, I charge thee, come out of him, and enter no more into him." And the spirit cried, and rent him sore, and came out of him: and he was as one dead; insomuch that many said, "He is dead." But Jesus took him by the hand, and lifted him up; and delivered him again to his father. And they were all amazed at the mighty power of God. And when he was come into the house, his disciples asked him privately, "Why could not we cast him out?" And Jesus said unto them, "Because of your unbelief: for verily I say unto you, If ye have faith as a grain of mustard-seed, ye shall say unto this mountain, Remove hence to yonder place; and it shall remove; and nothing shall be impossible unto you. Howbeit this kind goeth not out but by prayer and fasting."

And they departed thence, and passed through Galilee; and he would
He foretelleth his own death. not that any man should know it. For he taught his disciples, and said unto them, "Let these sayings sink down into your ears: for the Son of man shall be delivered into the hands of men, and they shall kill him; and after that he is killed, he shall rise the third day." But they understood not this saying, and it was hid from them, that they perceived it not: and they feared to ask him of that saying.

CHAPTER XX.

AND when they were come to Capernaum, they that received tribute money came to Peter, and said, Doth not your master pay tribute? He saith, Yes. And when he was come into the house, Jesus prevented him, saying, "What thinkest thou, Simon? of whom do the kings of the earth take custom or tribute? of their own children, or of strangers?" Peter saith unto him, "Of strangers." Jesus saith unto him, "Then are the children free. Notwithstanding, lest we should offend them, go thou to the sea, and cast an hook, and take up the fish that first cometh up: and when thou hast opened his mouth, thou shalt find a piece of money: that take, and give unto them for me and thee."

ROMAN TRIBUTE MONEY.

And being in the house he asked them, "What was it that ye disputed among yourselves by the way?" But they held their peace: for by the way they had disputed among themselves, who should be the greatest. And Jesus, perceiving the thought of their heart, sat down, and called the twelve, and saith unto them, "If any man desire to be first, the same shall be last of all, and servant of all." And he took a child, and set him in the midst of them: and when he had taken him in his arms, he said unto them, "Verily I say unto you, Except ye be converted, and become as little children, ye shall not enter into the kingdom of heaven. Whosoever therefore shall humble himself as this little child, the same is greatest in the kingdom of heaven. And whoso shall receive one such little child in my name receiveth me: and whosoever shall receive me, receiveth not me, but him that sent me."

And John answered him, saying, "Master, we saw one casting out devils in thy name, and he followeth not us: and we forbade him, because he

followeth not us." But Jesus said, "Forbid him not: for there is no man
which shall do a miracle in my name, that can lightly speak evil
of me. For he that is not against us is on our part. For whosoever shall give you a cup of water to drink in my name, because ye belong
to Christ, verily I say unto you, he shall not lose his reward. And whosoever shall offend one of these little ones that believe in me, it
is better for him that a millstone were hanged about his neck,
and he were cast into the sea. And if thy hand offend thee, cut it off: it is
better for thee to enter into life maimed, than having two hands to go into
hell, into the fire that never shall be quenched: where their worm dieth
not, and the fire is not quenched. And if thy foot offend thee, cut it off: it
is better for thee to enter halt into life, than having two feet to be cast into
hell, into the fire that never shall be quenched: where their worm dieth
not, and the fire is not quenched. And if thine eye offend thee, pluck it
out: it is better for thee to enter into the kingdom of God with one eye,
than having two eyes to be cast into hell-fire: where their worm dieth not,
and the fire is not quenched. For every one shall be salted with fire, and
every sacrifice shall be salted with salt. Salt is good: but if the salt have
lost his saltness, wherewith will ye season it? Have salt in yourselves, and
have peace one with another.

"Take heed that ye despise not one of these little ones; for I say
unto you, That in heaven their angels do always behold the
face of my Father which is in heaven. For the Son of man is
come to save that which was lost. How think ye? if a man have an hundred sheep, and one of them be gone astray, doth he not leave
the ninety and nine, and goeth into the mountains, and seeketh
that which is gone astray? and if so be that he find it, verily I say unto
you, he rejoiceth more of that sheep, than of the ninety and nine which
went not astray. Even so it is not the will of your Father which is in
heaven, that one of these little ones should perish.

"Moreover if thy brother shall trespass against thee, go and tell him his
fault between thee and him alone: if he shall hear thee, thou
hast gained thy brother. But if he will not hear thee, then take
with thee one or two more, that in the mouth of two or three witnesses
every word may be established. And if he shall neglect to hear them, tell
it unto the church: but if he neglect to hear the church, let him be unto
thee as an heathen man and a publican. Verily I say unto you, Whatsoever ye shall bind on earth shall be bound in heaven: and whatsoever ye
shall loose on earth shall be loosed in heaven. Again I say unto you, That
if two of you shall agree on earth as touching anything that
they shall ask, it shall be done for them of my Father which is
in heaven. For where two or three are gathered together in my name,
there am I in the midst of them."

Then came Peter to him, and said, "Lord, how oft shall my brother sin against me, and I forgive him? till seven times?" Jesus saith unto him, "I say not unto thee, Until seven times: but, Until seventy times seven. Therefore is the kingdom of heaven likened unto a certain king, which would take account of his servants. And when he had begun to reckon, one was brought unto him, which owed him ten thousand talents. But forasmuch as he had not to pay, his lord commanded him to be sold, and his wife, and children, and all that he had, and payment to be made. The servant therefore fell down, and worshiped him, saying, 'Lord, have patience with me, and I will pay thee all.' Then the lord of that servant was moved with compassion, and loosed him, and forgave him the debt. But the same servant went out, and found one of his fellow-servants, which owed him an hundred pence: and he laid hands on him, and took him by the throat, saying, 'Pay me that thou owest.' And his fellow-servant fell down at his feet, and besought him, saying, 'Have patience with me, and I will pay thee all.' And he would not: but went and cast him into prison, till he should pay the debt. So when his fellow-servants saw what was done, they were very sorry, and came and told unto their lord all that was done. Then his lord, after that he had called him, said unto him, 'O thou wicked servant, I forgave thee all that debt, because thou desiredst me: shouldest not thou also have had compassion on thy fellow-servant, even as I had pity on thee?' And his lord was wroth, and delivered him to the tormentors, till he should pay all that was due unto him. So likewise shall my heavenly Father do also unto you, if ye from your hearts forgive not every one his brother their trespasses."

The unforgiving servant.

CHAPTER XXI.

JESUS AT THE FEAST OF TABERNACLES.

OW the Jews' feast of tabernacles was at hand. His brethren therefore said unto him, "Depart hence, and go into Judæa, that thy disciples also may see the works that thou doest. For there is no man that doeth anything in secret, and he himself seeketh to be known openly. If thou do these things, show thyself to the world." For neither did his brethren believe in him. Then Jesus said unto His brethren urge him to attend the feast. them, "My time is not yet come: but your time is alway ready. The world cannot hate you: but me it hateth, because I testify of it, that the works thereof are evil. Go ye up unto this feast: I go not up yet unto this feast; for my time is not yet full come." When he had said these words unto them, he abode still in Galilee. But when his brethren were gone up, then went he also up unto the feast, not openly, but as it were in secret.

And it came to pass, when the time was come that he should be received up, he steadfastly set his face to go to Jerusalem. And it came to pass, as he went to Jerusalem, that he passed through the midst of Samaria and Galilee, and sent messengers before his face: and they went, and entered into a village of the Samaritans, to make ready for him. And they did not receive him, because his face was as though he would go to Jerusalem. And when his disciples James and John saw this, they said, "Lord, wilt thou that we command fire to come down from heaven, and Christ refuses to call fire from heaven. consume them, even as Elijah did?" But he turned, and rebuked them, and said, "Ye know not what manner of spirit ye are of. For the Son of man is not come to destroy men's lives, but to save them." And they went to another village.

And it came to pass, that as they went in the way, a certain scribe said unto him, "Lord, I will follow thee whithersoever thou goest." And Jesus said unto him, "Foxes have holes, and birds of the air have He instructs certain who wish to be his disciples. nests: but the Son of man hath not where to lay his head." And he said unto another, "Follow me." But he said, "Lord, suffer me first to go and bury my father." Jesus said unto him, "Let the dead bury their dead: but go thou and preach the kingdom of God." And another also said, "Lord, I will follow thee; but let me first go bid them farewell, which are at home at my house." And Jesus said unto him, "No man, having put his hand to the plow, and looking back, is fit for the kingdom of God."

Then the Jews sought him at the feast, and said, "Where is he?" And *The people seek him at the feast.* there was much murmuring among the people concerning him: for some said, "He is a good man": others said, "Nay; but he deceiveth the people." Howbeit no man spake openly of him for fear of the Jews.

Now about the midst of the feast Jesus went up into the temple, and taught. And the Jews marveled, saying, "How knoweth this man letters, *Jesus appears at the feast.* having never learned?" Jesus answered them, and said, "My doctrine is not mine, but his that sent me. If any man will do his will, he shall know of the doctrine, whether it be of God, or whether I speak of myself. He that speaketh of himself seeketh his own glory: but he that seeketh his glory that sent him, the same is true, and no unrighteousness is in him. Did not Moses give you the law, and yet none of you keepeth the law? Why go ye about to kill me?" The people answered and said, "Thou hast a devil: who goeth about to kill thee?" Jesus answered and said unto them, "I have done one work, and ye all marvel. Moses therefore gave unto you circumcision; (not because it is of Moses, but of the fathers;) and ye on the sabbath day circumcise a man. If a man on the sabbath day receive circumcision, that the law of Moses should not be broken; are ye angry at me, because I have made a man every whit whole on the sabbath day? Judge not according to the appearance, but judge righteous judgment." Then said some of them of Jerusalem, "Is not this he, whom they seek to kill? but, lo, he speaketh boldly, and they say nothing unto him. Do the rulers know indeed that this is the very Christ? howbeit we know this man whence he is: but when Christ cometh, no man knoweth whence he is." Then cried Jesus in the temple as he taught, saying, "Ye both know me, and ye know whence I am: and I am not come of myself, but he that sent me is true, whom ye know not. But I know him: for I am from him, and he hath sent me."

Then they sought to take him: but no man laid hands on him, because *Many believe on him.* his hour was not yet come. And many of the people believed on him, and said, "When Christ cometh, will he do more miracles than these which this man hath done?" The Pharisees heard that the people murmured such things concerning him; and the Pharisees and the chief priests sent officers to take him.

Then said Jesus unto them, "Yet a little while am I with you, and then I go unto him that sent me. Ye shall seek me, and shall not find me: and where I am, thither ye cannot come." *He foretelleth his death.*

Then said the Jews among themselves, "Whither will he go, that we shall not find him? will he go unto the dispersed among the Gentiles, and teach the Gentiles? what manner of saying is this that he said, Ye shall seek me, and shall not find me: and where I am, thither ye cannot come?"

In the last day, that great day of the feast, Jesus stood and cried, saying, "If any man thirst, let him come unto me, and drink. He that believeth on me, as the scripture hath said, out of his belly *He offereth the water of life.* shall flow rivers of living water." (But this spake he of the Spirit, which they that believe on him should receive: for the Holy Ghost was not yet given; because that Jesus was not yet glorified.)

Many of the people therefore, when they heard this saying, said, "Of a truth this is the Prophet." Others said, "This is the Christ." *The people dispute about him.* But some said, "Shall Christ come out of Galilee? hath not the scripture said, that Christ cometh of the seed of David, and out of the town of Bethlehem, where David was?" So there was a division among the people because of him. And some of them would have taken him; but no man laid hands on him.

Then came the officers to the chief priests and Pharisees: and they said unto them, "Why have ye not brought him?" The officers *The officers testify of him.* answered, "Never man spake like this man." Then answered them the Pharisees, "Are ye also deceived? Have any of the rulers or of the Pharisees believed on him? but this people who knoweth not the law are cursed." Nicodemus saith unto them, (he that came to Jesus by night, being one of them,) "Doth our law judge any *Nicodemus pleads for him.* man before it hear him, and know what he doeth?" They answered and said unto him, "Art thou also of Galilee? Search, and look: for out of Galilee ariseth no prophet." And every man went unto his own house. And Jesus went unto the mount of Olives.

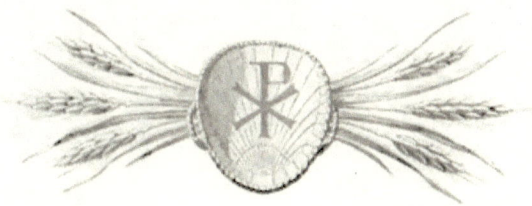

SERVANTS OF THE CHIEF PRIEST

CHAPTER XXII

DISCUSSIONS WITH THE PHARISEES.

 ND early in the morning he came again into the temple, and all the people came unto him; and he sat down, and taught them. And the scribes and Pharisees brought unto him a woman taken in adultery; and when they had set her in the midst, they say unto him, "Master, this woman was taken in adultery, in the very act. Now The woman taken in adultery. Moses in the law commanded us, that such should be stoned: but what sayest thou?" This they said, tempting him, that they might have to accuse him.

But Jesus stooped down, and with his finger wrote on the ground, as though he heard them not. So when they continued asking him, he lifted up himself, and said unto them, "He that is without sin among you, let him first cast a stone at her." And again he stooped down, and wrote on the ground. And they which heard it, being convicted by their own conscience, went out one by one, beginning at the eldest, even unto the last: and Jesus was left alone, and the woman standing in the midst. When Jesus had lifted up himself, and saw none but the woman, he said unto her, "Woman, where are those thine accusers? hath no man condemned thee?" She said, "No man, Lord." And Jesus said unto her, "Neither do I condemn thee: go, and sin no more."

Then spake Jesus again unto them, saying, "I am the light of the world: he that followeth me shall not walk in darkness, but shall have Jesus the light of the world. the light of life." The Pharisees therefore said unto him, "Thou bearest record of thyself; thy record is not true." Jesus answered and said unto them, "Though I bear record of myself, yet my record is true: for I know whence I came, and whither I go: but ye cannot tell whence I come, and whither I go. Ye judge after the flesh; I judge no man. He rebukes the Pharisees and disputes with them. And yet if I judge, my judgment is true: for I am not alone, but I and the Father that sent me. It is also written in your law, that the testimony of two men is true. I am one that bear witness of myself, and the Father that sent me beareth witness of me." Then said they unto him,

THE WOMAN TAKEN IN ADULTERY.

"Where is thy Father?" Jesus answered, "Ye neither know me, nor my Father: if ye had known me, ye should have known my Father also." These words spake Jesus in the treasury, as he taught in the temple: and no man laid hands on him; for his hour was not yet come.

Then said Jesus again unto them, "I go my way, and ye shall seek me, and shall die in your sins: whither I go, ye cannot come." Then said the Jews, "Will he kill himself? because he saith, Whither I go, ye cannot come." And he said unto them, "Ye are from beneath; I am from above: ye are of this world; I am not of this world. I said therefore unto you, that ye shall die in your sins: for if ye believe not that I am he, ye shall die in your sins."

Then said they unto him, "Who art thou?" And Jesus saith unto them, "Even the same that I said unto you from the beginning. I have many things to say and to judge of you: but he that sent me is true; and I speak to the world those things which I have heard of him." They understood not that he spake to them of the Father. Then said Jesus unto them, "When ye have lifted up the Son of man, then shall ye know that I am he, and that I do nothing of myself; but as my Father hath taught me, I speak these things. And he that sent me is with me: the Father hath not left me alone; for I do always those things that please him."

As he spake these words, many believed on him. Then said Jesus to those Jews which believed on him, "If ye continue in my word, then are ye my disciples indeed; and ye shall know the truth, and the truth shall make you free." They answered him, "We be Abraham's seed, and were never in bondage to any man: how sayest thou, Ye shall be made free?" Jesus answered them, "Verily, verily, I say unto you, Whosoever committeth sin is the servant of sin. And the servant abideth not in the house forever: but the Son abideth ever. If the Son therefore shall make you free, ye shall be free indeed. I know that ye are Abraham's seed; but ye seek to kill me, because my word hath no place in you. I speak that which I have seen with my Father: and ye do that which ye have seen with your father." They answered and said unto him, Abraham is our father. Jesus saith unto them, "If ye were Abraham's children, ye would do the works of Abraham. But now ye seek to kill me, a man that hath told you the truth, which I have heard of God: this did not Abraham. Ye do the deeds of your father." Then said they to him, "We be not born of fornication; we have one Father, even God."

Jesus said unto them, "If God were your Father, ye would love me: for I proceeded forth and came from God; neither came I of myself, but he sent me. Why do ye not understand my speech? even because ye cannot hear my word. Ye are of your father the devil, and the lusts of your father ye will do. He was a murderer from the beginning, and abode not in the truth, because there is no truth in him. When he speaketh a lie, he speaketh of his own: for he is a liar, and the father of it. And because I tell you the truth, ye believe me not. Which of you convinceth me of sin? And if I say the truth, why do ye not believe me? He that is of God heareth God's words: ye therefore hear them not, because ye are not of God."

Then answered the Jews, and said unto him, "Say we not well that thou art a Samaritan, and hast a devil?" Jesus answered, "I have not a devil; but I honor my Father, and ye do dishonor me. And I seek not mine own glory: there is one that seeketh and judgeth. Verily, verily, I say unto you, If a man keep my saying, he shall never see death." Then said the Jews unto him, "Now we know that thou hast a devil. Abraham is dead, and the prophets; and thou sayest, If a man keep my saying, he shall never taste of death. Art thou greater than our father Abraham, which is dead? and the prophets are dead: whom makest thou thyself?"

Jesus answered, "If I honor myself, my honor is nothing: it is my Father that honoreth me; of whom ye say, that he is your God: yet ye have not known him; but I know him: and if I should say, I know him not, I shall be a liar like unto you: but I know him, and keep his saying. Your father Abraham rejoiced to see my day: and he saw it, and was glad." *Jesus declareth his own eternity.* Then said the Jews unto him, "Thou art not yet fifty years old, and hast thou seen Abraham?" Jesus said unto them, "Verily, verily, I say unto you, Before Abraham was, I am."

They try to stone him. Then took they up stones to cast at him: but Jesus hid himself, and went out of the temple, going through the midst of them, and so passed by.

CHAPTER XXIII.

AND as Jesus passed by, he saw a man which was blind from his birth. And his disciples asked him, saying, "Master, who did sin, this man, or his parents, that he was born blind?" Jesus answered, "Neither hath this man sinned, nor his parents: but that the works of God should be made manifest in him. I must work the works of him that sent me, while it is day: the night cometh, when no man can work. As long as I am in the world, I am the light of the world." When he had thus spoken, he spat on the ground, and made clay of the spittle, and he anointed the eyes of the blind man with the clay, and said unto him, "Go, wash in the pool of Siloam," (which is by interpretation, Sent.) He went his way therefore, and washed, and came seeing. The neighbors therefore, and they which before had seen him that he was blind, said, "Is not this he that sat and begged?" Some said, "This is he"; others said, "He is like him"; but he said, "I am he." Therefore said they unto him, "How were thine eyes opened?" He answered and said, "A man that is called Jesus made clay, and anointed mine eyes, and said unto me, Go to the pool of Siloam, and wash: and I went and washed, and I received sight." Then said they unto him, "Where is he?" He said, "I know not."

The man born blind receives his sight.

Then they brought to the Pharisees him that aforetime was blind. And it was the sabbath day when Jesus made the clay, and opened his eyes. The Pharisees also asked him how he had received his sight. He said unto them, "He put clay upon mine eyes, and I washed, and do see." Therefore said some of the Pharisees, "This man is not of God, because he keepeth not the sabbath day." Others said, "How can a man that is a sinner do such miracles?" And there was a division among them. They say unto the blind man again, "What sayest thou of him, that he hath opened thine eyes?" He said, "He is a prophet."

But the Jews did not believe concerning him, that he had been blind,

and received his sight, until they called the parents of him that had received his sight. And they asked them, saying, "Is this your son, who ye say was born blind? how then doth he now see?" His parents *The man is excommunicated* answered them and said, "We know that this is our son, and that he was born blind: but by what means he now seeth, we know not; or who hath opened his eyes, we know not: he is of age; ask him: he shall speak for himself." These words spake his parents, because they feared the Jews: for the Jews had agreed already, that if any man did confess that he was Christ, he should be put out of the synagogue. Therefore said his parents, "He is of age; ask him."

Then again called they the man that was blind, and said unto him, "Give God the praise: we know that this man is a sinner." He answered and said, "Whether he be a sinner or no, I know not: one thing I know, that, whereas I was blind, now I see." Then said they to him again, "What did he to thee? how opened he thine eyes?" He answered them, "I have told you already, and ye did not hear: wherefore would ye hear it again? will ye also be his disciples?" Then they reviled him, and said, "Thou art his disciple; but we are Moses' disciples. We know that God spake unto Moses: as for this fellow, we know not from whence he is."

The man answered and said unto them, "Why herein is a marvelous thing, that ye know not from whence he is, and yet he hath opened mine eyes. Now we know that God heareth not sinners: but if any man be a worshiper of God, and doeth his will, him he heareth. Since the world began was it not heard that any man opened the eyes of one that was born blind. If this man were not of God, he could do nothing." They answered and said unto him, "Thou wast altogether born in sins, and dost thou teach us?" And they cast him out.

Jesus heard that they had cast him out; and when he had found him, he said unto him, "Dost thou believe on the Son of God?" He answered and said, "Who is he, Lord, that I might believe on him?" And Jesus said unto him, "Thou hast both seen him, and it is he that talketh *Jesus instructs him that was blind.* with thee." And he said, "Lord, I believe." And he worshiped him. And Jesus said, "For judgment I am come into this world, that they which see not might see; and that they which see might be made blind."

And some of the Pharisees which were with him heard these words, and said unto him, "Are we blind also?" Jesus said unto them, "If ye were blind, ye should have no sin: but now ye say, We see; therefore your sin remaineth."

"Verily, verily, I say unto you, He that entereth not by the door into the sheepfold, but climbeth up some other way, the same is a thief and a robber. But he that entereth in by the door is the shepherd of the sheep.

To him the porter openeth; and the sheep hear his voice: and he calleth his
Jesus the door and the shepherd of the sheep. own sheep by name, and leadeth them out. And when he putteth forth his own sheep, he goeth before them, and the sheep
follow him: for they know his voice. And a stranger will they not follow,
but will flee from him: for
they know not the voice of
strangers." This parable spake
Jesus unto them : but they
understood not what things
they were which he spake
unto them.

Then said Jesus unto them
again, "Verily, verily, I say
unto you, I am the door of the
sheep. All that ever came
before me are thieves and
robbers : but the sheep did
not hear them. I am the door :
by me, if any man enter in, he shall be saved, and shall go in and out, and
find pasture. The thief cometh not, but for to steal, and to kill, and to
destroy : I am come that they might have life, and that they might have it
more abundantly. I am the good shepherd: the good shepherd giveth his
life for the sheep. But he that is an hireling, and not the shepherd, whose
own the sheep are not, seeth the wolf coming, and leaveth the sheep, and
fleeth : and the wolf catcheth them, and scattereth the sheep. The hireling
fleeth, because he is an hireling, and careth not for the sheep. I am the
good shepherd, and know my sheep, and am known of mine. As the Father
knoweth me, even so know I the Father : and I lay down my life for the
sheep. And other sheep I have, which are not of this fold: them also I
must bring, and they shall hear my voice ; and there shall be one fold, and
one shepherd. Therefore doth my Father love me, because I lay down my
life, that I might take it again. No man taketh it from me, but I lay it
down of myself. I have power to lay it down, and I have power to take it
again. This commandment have I received of my Father.

There was a division therefore again among the Jews for these sayings.
The council is divided. And many of them said, "He hath a devil, and is mad ; why
hear ye him ?" Others said, "These are not the words of him
that hath a devil. Can a devil open the eyes of the blind ?"

"PEACE BE TO THIS HOUSE."

CHAPTER XXIV.

THE SENDING OF THE SEVENTY, WITH OTHER INCIDENTS.

AFTER these things the Lord appointed other seventy also, and sent them two and two before his face into every city and place, whither he himself would come. Therefore said he unto them, "The harvest truly is great, but the laborers are few: pray ye therefore the Lord of the harvest, that he would send forth laborers into his harvest. Go your ways: behold, I send you forth as lambs among wolves. Carry neither purse, nor scrip, nor shoes: and salute no man by the way. And into whatsoever house ye enter, first say, Peace be to this house. And if the son of peace be there, your peace shall rest upon it: if not, it shall turn to you again. And in the same house remain, eating and drinking such things as they give: for the laborer is worthy of his hire. Go not from house to house. And into whatsoever city ye enter, and they receive you, eat such things as are set before you: and heal the sick that are therein, and say unto them, The kingdom of God is come nigh unto you. But into whatsoever city ye enter, and they receive you not, go your ways out into the streets of the same, and say, Even the very dust of your city, which cleaveth on us, we do wipe off against you: notwithstanding be ye sure of this, that the kingdom of God is come nigh unto you. But I say unto you, that it shall be more tolerable in that day for Sodom, than for that city.

SITTING IN SACKCLOTH AND ASHES

"Woe unto thee, Chorazin! woe unto thee, Bethsaida! for if the mighty works had been done in Tyre and Sidon, which have been done in you, they had a great while ago repented, sitting in sackcloth and ashes. But it shall be more tolerable for Tyre and Sidon at the judgment, than for you. And thou, Capernaum, which art exalted to heaven, shalt be thrust down to hell. He that heareth you heareth me:

and he that despiseth you despiseth me; and he that despiseth me despiseth him that sent me."

And the seventy returned again with joy, saying, "Lord, even the devils are subject unto us through thy name." And he said unto them, "I beheld Satan as lightning fall from heaven. Behold, I give unto you power to tread on serpents and scorpions, and over all the power of the enemy: and nothing shall by any means hurt you. Notwithstanding in this rejoice not, that the spirits are subject unto you; but rather rejoice, because your names are written in heaven."

The seventy return.

In that hour Jesus rejoiced in spirit, and said, "I thank thee, O Father, Lord of heaven and earth, that thou hast hid these things from the wise and prudent, and hast revealed them unto babes: even so, Father; for so it seemed good in thy sight. All things are delivered to me of my Father: and no man knoweth who the Son is, but the Father; and who the Father is, but the Son, and he to whom the Son will reveal him." And he turned him unto his disciples, and said privately, "Blessed are the eyes which see the things that ye see: for I tell you, that many prophets and kings have desired to see those things which ye see, and have not seen them; and to hear those things which ye hear, and have not heard them."

Jesus rejoices.

And, behold, a certain lawyer stood up, and tempted him, saying, "Master, what shall I do to inherit eternal life?" He said unto him, "What is written in the law? how readest thou?" And he answering said, "Thou shalt love the Lord thy God with all thy heart, and with all thy soul, and with all thy strength, and with all thy mind; and thy neighbor as thyself." And he said unto him, "Thou hast answered right: this do, and thou shalt live." But he, willing to justify himself, said unto Jesus, "And who is my neighbor?"

Who is my neighbor?

And Jesus answering said, "A certain man went down from Jerusalem to Jericho, and fell among thieves, which stripped him of his raiment, and wounded him, and departed, leaving him half dead. And by chance there came down a certain priest that way: and when he saw him, he passed by on the other side. And likewise a Levite, when he was at the place, came and looked on him, and passed by on the other side. But a certain Samaritan, as he journeyed, came where he was: and when he saw him, he had compassion on him, and went to him, and bound up his wounds, pouring in oil and wine, and set him on his own beast, and brought him to an inn, and took care of him. And on the morrow when he departed, he took out two pence, and gave them to the host, and said unto

The good Samaritan.

THE GOOD SAMARITAN AT THE INN.

him, Take care of him; and whatsoever thou spendest more, when I come again, I will repay thee. Which now of these three, thinkest thou, was neighbor unto him that fell among the thieves?" And he said, "He that showed mercy on him." Then said Jesus unto him, "Go, and do thou likewise."

Now it came to pass, as they went, that he entered into a certain village:

Mary sits at Jesus' feet.

and a certain woman named Martha received him into her house. And she had a sister called Mary, which also sat at Jesus' feet, and heard his word. But Martha was cumbered about much serving, and came to him, and said, "Lord, dost thou not care that my sister hath left me to serve alone? bid her therefore that she help me." And Jesus answered and said unto her, "Martha, Martha, thou art careful and troubled about many things: but one thing is needful: and Mary hath chosen that good part, which shall not be taken away from her."

And it came to pass, as he was praying in a certain place, when he ceased, one of his disciples said unto him, "Lord, teach us to pray, as John also taught his disciples." And he said unto them, "When ye pray, say, Our Father which art in heaven, Hallowed be thy name. Thy kingdom

Christ teaches to pray.

come. Thy will be done, as in heaven, so in earth. Give us day by day our daily bread. And forgive us our sins; for we also forgive every one that is indebted to us. And lead us not into temptation; but deliver us from evil."

And he said unto them, "Which of you shall have a friend, and shall go unto him at midnight, and say unto him, Friend, lend me three loaves; for a friend of mine in his journey is come to me, and I have nothing to set before him? And he from within shall answer and say, Trouble me not: the door is now shut, and my children are with me in bed; I cannot rise and give thee. I say unto you, Though he will not rise and give him,

The importunate friend.

because he is his friend, yet because of his importunity he will rise and give him as many as he needeth. And I say unto you, Ask, and it shall be given you; seek, and ye shall find; knock, and it shall be opened unto you. For every one that asketh receiveth; and he that seeketh findeth; and to him that knocketh it shall be opened. If a son shall ask bread of any of you that is a father, will he give him a stone? or if he ask a fish, will he for a fish give him a serpent? or if he shall ask an egg, will he offer him a scorpion? If ye then, being evil, know how to give good gifts unto your children, how much more shall your heavenly Father give the Holy Spirit to them that ask him?"

And he was teaching in one of the synagogues on the sabbath. And, behold, there was a woman which had a spirit of infirmity eighteen years, and was bowed together, and could in no wise lift up herself. And when Jesus saw her, he called her to him, and said unto her, "Woman, thou art loosed

from thine infirmity." And he laid his hands on her: and immediately she was made straight, and glorified God. And the ruler of the synagogue

He healeth an infirm woman. answered with indignation, because that Jesus had healed on the sabbath day, and said unto the people, "There are six days in which men ought to work: in them therefore come and be healed, and not on the sabbath day." The Lord then answered him, and said, "Thou hypocrite, doth not each one of you on the sabbath loose his ox or his ass from the stall, and lead him away to watering? and ought not this woman, being a daughter of Abraham, whom Satan hath bound, lo, these eighteen years, be loosed from this bond on the sabbath day?" And when he had said these things, all his adversaries were ashamed: and all the people rejoiced for all the glorious things that were done by him.

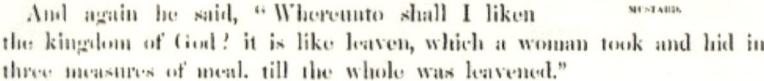

Then said he, "Unto what is the kingdom of God like? and whereunto shall I resemble it? it is like a grain of mustard-seed, which a man took, and cast into his garden; and it grew, and waxed a great tree; and the fowls of the air lodged in the branches of it."

And again he said, "Whereunto shall I liken

MUSTARD.

the kingdom of God? it is like leaven, which a woman took and hid in three measures of meal, till the whole was leavened."

HEALING OF AN AGED WOMAN.

CHAPTER XXV.

AND he was casting out a devil, and it was dumb. And it came to pass, when the devil was gone out, the dumb spake: and the people wondered. But some of them said, "He casteth out devils through Beelzebub the chief of the devils." And others, tempting him, sought of him a sign from heaven. But he, knowing their thoughts, said unto them, "Every kingdom divided against itself is brought to desolation; and a house divided against a house falleth. If Satan also be divided against himself, how shall his kingdom stand? because ye say that I cast out devils through Beelzebub. And if I by Beelzebub cast out devils, by whom do your sons cast them out? therefore shall they be your judges. But if I with the finger of God cast out devils, no doubt the kingdom of God is come upon you. When a strong man armed keepeth his palace, his goods are in peace: but when a stronger than he shall come upon him, and overcome him, he taketh from him all his armor wherein he trusted, and divideth his spoils. He that is not with me is against me: and he that gathereth not with me scattereth. When the unclean spirit is gone out of a man, he walketh through dry places, seeking rest; and finding none, he saith, I will return unto my house whence I came out. And when he cometh, he findeth it swept and garnished. Then goeth he, and taketh to him seven other spirits more wicked than himself; and they enter in, and dwell there: and the last state of that man is worse than the first."

The Pharisees blaspheme.

And it came to pass, as he spake these things, a certain woman of the company lifted up her voice, and said unto him, "Blessed is the womb that bare thee, and the paps which thou hast sucked." But he said, "Yea rather, blessed are they that hear the word of God, and keep it."

Who are blessed.

And when the people were gathered thick together, he began to say, "An evil and adulterous generation seeketh after a sign: and there shall no sign be given to it, but the sign of the prophet Jonas: for as Jonas was three days and three nights in the whale's belly,

He rebuketh the Pharisees for seeking a sign from heaven.

so shall the Son of man be three days and three nights in the heart of the earth. The men of Nineveh shall rise in judgment with this generation, and shall condemn it: because they repented at the preaching of Jonas; and, behold, a greater than Jonas is here. The queen of the south shall rise up in the judgment with this generation, and shall condemn it: for she came from the uttermost parts of the earth to hear the wisdom of Solomon; and, behold, a greater than Solomon is here."

"No man, when he hath lighted a candle, putteth it in a secret place, neither under a bushel, but on a candlestick, that they which come in may see the light. The light of the body is the eye: therefore when thine eye is single, thy whole body also is full of light; but when thine eye is evil, thy body also is full of darkness. Take heed therefore that the light which is in thee be not darkness. If thy whole body therefore be full of light, having no part dark, the whole shall be full of light, as when the bright shining of a candle doth give thee light.

"When the unclean spirit is gone out of a man, he walketh through dry places, seeking rest, and findeth none. Then he saith, I will return into my house from whence I came out; and when he is come, he *The evil spirit that returned.* findeth it empty, swept, and garnished. Then goeth he, and taketh with himself seven other spirits more wicked than himself, and they enter in and dwell there: and the last state of that man is worse than the first. Even so shall it be also unto this wicked generation."

While he yet talked to the people, behold, his mother and his brethren stood without, desiring to speak with him. And they could not come at him for the press. Then one said unto him, "Behold, thy mother and thy brethren stand without, desiring to speak with thee." But he *Christ declares who are his brethren.* answered and said unto him that told him, "Who is my mother? and who are my brethren?" And he stretched forth his hand toward his disciples, and said, "Behold my mother and my brethren! For whosoever shall do the will of my Father which is in heaven, the same is my brother, and sister, and mother."

And as he spake, a certain Pharisee besought him to dine with him: and he went in, and sat down to meat. And when the Pharisee saw it, he marveled that he had not first washed before dinner. And the Lord said unto him, "Now do ye Pharisees make clean the outside of the cup *Reasoneth concerning washings.* and the platter; but your inward part is full of ravening and wickedness. Ye fools, did not he that made that which is without make that which is within also? but rather give alms of such things as ye have; and, behold, all things are clean unto you. But woe unto you, Pharisees! for ye tithe mint and rue and all manner of herbs, and pass over *Rebuketh the Pharisees and lawyers.* judgment and the love of God: these ought ye to have done, and not to leave the other undone. Woe unto you, Pharisees! for ye love

JESUS CONVERSES WITH THE DOCTORS OF THE LAW.

the uppermost seats in the synagogues, and greetings in the markets. Woe unto you, scribes and Pharisees, hypocrites! for ye are as graves which appear not, and the men that walk over them are not aware of them."

Then answered one of the lawyers, and said unto him, "Master, thus saying thou reproachest us also." And he said, "Woe unto you also, ye lawyers! for ye lade men with burdens grievous to be borne, and ye yourselves touch not the burdens with one of your fingers. Woe unto you! for ye build the sepulchers of the prophets, and your fathers killed them. Truly ye bear witness that ye allow the deeds of your fathers: for they indeed killed them, and ye build their sepulchers. Therefore also said the wisdom of God, I will send them prophets and apostles, and some of them they shall slay and persecute: that the blood of all the prophets, which was shed from the foundation of the world, may be required of this generation; from the blood of Abel unto the blood of Zacharias, which perished between the altar and the temple: verily I say unto you, It shall be required of this generation. Woe unto you, lawyers! for ye have taken away the key of knowledge: ye entered not in yourselves, and them that were entering in ye hindered."

And as he said these things unto them, the scribes and the Pharisees began to urge him vehemently, and to provoke him to speak of many things: laying wait for him, and seeking to catch something out of his mouth, that they might accuse him.

CHAPTER XXVI.

IN the mean time, when there were gathered together an innumerable multitude of people, insomuch that they trode one upon another, he began to say unto his disciples first of all, "Beware ye of the leaven of the Pharisees, which is hypocrisy. For there is nothing covered, that shall not be revealed; neither hid, that shall not be known. Therefore whatsoever ye have spoken in darkness shall be heard in the light; and that which ye have spoken in the ear in closets shall be proclaimed upon the house-tops. And I say unto you, my friends, Be not afraid of

Not to fear men. them that kill the body, and after that have no more that they can do. But I will forewarn you whom ye shall fear: Fear him, which after he hath killed hath power to cast into hell; yea, I say unto you, Fear him.

"Are not five sparrows sold for two farthings, and not one of them is forgotten before God? But even the very hairs of your head are all numbered. Fear not therefore: ye are of more value than many sparrows. Also I say unto you, Whosoever shall confess me before men,

Of God's care. him shall the Son of man also confess before the angels of God: but he that denieth me before men shall be denied before the angels of God. And when they bring you unto the synagogues, and unto magistrates, and powers, take ye no thought how or what thing ye shall answer, or what ye shall say: for the Holy Ghost shall teach you in the same hour what ye ought to say."

And one of the company said unto him, "Master, speak to my brother, that he divide the inheritance with me." And he said unto him, "Man,

Against covetousness. who made me a judge or a divider over you?" And he said unto them, "Take heed, and beware of covetousness: for a man's life consisteth not in the abundance of the things which he possesseth."

And he spake a parable unto them, saying, "The ground of a certain

156

rich man brought forth plentifully; and he thought within himself, saying, What shall I do, because I have no room where to bestow my fruits? And he said, This will I do: I will pull down my barns, and build greater; and there will I bestow all my fruits and my goods. And I will say to my soul, Soul, thou hast much goods laid up for many years: take thine ease, eat, drink, and be merry. But God said unto him, Thou fool, this night thy soul shall be required of thee: then whose shall those things be, which thou hast provided? So is he that layeth up treasure for himself, and is not rich toward God."

The parable of the rich fool.

And he said unto his disciples, "Therefore I say unto you, Take no thought for your life, what ye shall eat; neither for the body, what ye shall put on. The life is more than meat, and the body is more than raiment. Consider

Of thought-taking.

LILIES OF PALESTINE.

the ravens: for they neither sow nor reap; which neither have storehouse nor barn; and God feedeth them: how much more are ye better than the fowls? And which of you with taking thought can add to his stature one cubit? If ye then be not able to do that thing which is least, why take ye thought for the rest? Consider the lilies how they grow: they toil not, they spin not; and yet I say unto you, that Solomon in all his glory was not arrayed like one of these. If then God so clothe the grass, which is to-day in the field, and to-morrow is cast into the oven; how much more will he clothe you, O ye of little faith? And seek not ye what ye shall eat, or what ye shall drink, neither be ye of doubtful mind. For all these things do the nations of the world seek after: and your Father knoweth that ye have need of these things. But rather seek ye the kingdom of God; and all these things shall be added unto you. Fear not, little flock; for it is your Father's good pleasure to give you the kingdom.

"Sell that ye have, and give alms: provide yourselves bags which wax not old, a treasure in the heavens that faileth not, where no thief approacheth, neither moth corrupteth. For where your treasure is, there will your heart be also. Let your loins be girded about, and your lights burning, and ye yourselves like unto men that wait for their lord, when he will return from the wedding: that when he cometh and

Of laying up treasure in heaven.

knocketh, they may open unto him immediately. Blessed are those servants, whom the lord when he cometh shall find watching:
Of watchfulness.
verily I say unto you, that he shall gird himself, and make them
to sit down to meat, and will come forth and serve them. And if he shall
come in the second watch, or come in the third watch, and find them
so, blessed are those servants. And this know, that if the good man of
the house had known what hour the thief would come, he would have
watched, and not have suffered his house to be broken through. Be ye
therefore ready also: for the Son of man cometh at an hour when ye think
not."

Then Peter said unto him, "Lord, speakest thou this parable unto us, or
even to all?" And the Lord said, "Who then is that faithful and wise
steward, whom his lord shall make ruler over his household, to give them
their portion of meat in due season? Blessed is that servant whom his lord
when he cometh shall find so doing. Of a truth I say unto you, that he
will make him ruler over all that he hath. But and if that servant say in
his heart, My lord delayeth his coming; and shall begin to beat the men-
servants and maidens, and to eat and drink, and to be drunken; the lord
of that servant will come in a day when he looketh not for him, and at an
hour when he is not aware, and will cut him in sunder, and will appoint
him his portion with the unbelievers. And that servant which knew his
lord's will, and prepared not himself, neither did according to his will, shall
be beaten with many stripes. But he that knew not, and did commit things
worthy of stripes, shall be beaten with few stripes. For unto whomsoever
much is given, of him shall be much required: and to whom men have
committed much, of him they will ask the more.

"I am come to send fire on the earth; and what will I, if it be already
kindled? but I have a baptism to be baptized with; and how am I
straitened till it be accomplished? Suppose ye that I am come to give
The religion of   peace on earth? I tell you, Nay; but rather division: for
Christ causes
division.   from henceforth there shall be five in one house divided,
three against two, and two against three. The father shall be divided
against the son, and the son against the father; the mother against
the daughter, and the daughter against the mother; the mother-in-law
against her daughter-in-law, and the daughter-in-law against her mother-
in-law."

And he said also to the people, "When ye see a cloud rise out of the
Of the signs of the   west, straightway ye say, There cometh a shower; and so
time.   it is. And when ye see the south-wind blow, ye say, There
will be heat; and it cometh to pass. Ye hypocrites, ye can discern the
face of the sky and of the earth; but how is it that ye do not discern
this time?

"Yea, and why even of yourselves judge ye not what is right? When thou goest with thine adversary to the magistrate, as thou art in the way, give diligence that thou mayest be delivered from him; lest he hale thee to the judge, and the judge deliver thee to the officer, and the officer cast thee into prison. I tell thee, thou shalt not depart thence, till thou hast paid the very last mite." *Of agreeing with the adversary*

There were present at that season some that told him of the Galileans, whose blood Pilate had mingled with their sacrifices. And Jesus answering said unto them, "Suppose ye that these Galileans were sinners above all the Galileans, because they suffered such things? I tell you, Nay: but, except ye repent, ye shall all likewise perish. Or those eighteen, upon whom the tower in Siloam fell, and slew them, think ye that they were sinners above all men that dwelt in Jerusalem? I tell you, Nay: but, except ye repent, ye shall all likewise perish." *The Galileans slain by Pilate.*

He spake also this parable: "A certain man had a fig-tree planted in his vineyard; and he came and sought fruit thereon, and found none. Then said he unto the dresser of his vineyard, Behold, these three years I come seeking fruit on this fig-tree, and find none: cut it down; why cumbereth it the ground? And he answering said unto him, Lord, let it alone this year also, till I shall dig about it, and dung it: and if it bear fruit, well: and if not, then after that thou shalt cut it down." *Parable of the unfruitful fig-tree.*

CHAPTER XXVII.

AT THE FEAST OF DEDICATION, AND BEYOND JORDAN.

AND it was at Jerusalem the feast of the dedication, and it was winter. And Jesus walked in the temple in Solomon's porch. Then came the Jews round about him, and said unto him, "How long dost thou make us to doubt? If thou be the Christ, tell us plainly." Jesus answered them, "I told you, and ye believed not: the works that I do in my Father's name, they bear witness of me. But ye believe not, because He declareth himself to be the Son of God. ye are not of my sheep, as I said unto you. My sheep hear my voice, and I know them, and they follow me: and I give unto them eternal life; and they shall never perish, neither shall any man pluck them out of my hand. My Father, which gave them me, is greater than all; and no man is able to pluck them out of my Father's hand. I and my Father are one."

Then the Jews took up stones again to stone him. Jesus answered them, "Many good works have I showed you from my Father; for which of The Jews seek to stone him. those works do ye stone me?" The Jews answered him, saying, "For a good work we stone thee not; but for blasphemy; and because that thou, being a man, makest thyself God." Jesus answered them, "Is it not written in your law, I said, Ye are gods? If he called them gods, unto whom the word of God came, and the scripture cannot be broken; say ye of him, whom the Father hath sanctified, and sent into the world, Thou blasphemest; because I said, I am the Son of God? If I do not the works of my Father, believe me not. But if I do, though ye believe not me, believe the works: that ye may know, and believe, that the Father is in me, and I in him." Therefore they sought again to take him: but he escaped out of their hand.

And he went away again beyond Jordan into the place where John at He retires beyond Jordan. first baptized; and there he abode. And great multitudes followed him, and said, "John did no miracle: but all things that John spake of this man were true." And many believed on him there. And as he was wont he taught them again and healed them.

And he went through the cities and villages, teaching, and journeying toward Jerusalem. Then said one unto him, "Lord, are there few that be saved?" And he said unto them, "Strive to enter in at the strait gate: for many, I say unto you, will seek to enter in, and shall not be able. When once the master of the house is risen up, and hath shut to the door, and ye begin to stand without, and to knock at the door, saying, Lord, Lord, open unto us: and he shall answer and say unto you, I know you not whence ye are: then shall ye begin to say, We have eaten and drunk in thy presence, and thou hast taught in our streets. But he shall say, I tell you, I know you not whence ye are; depart from me, all ye workers of iniquity. There shall be weeping and gnashing of teeth, when ye shall see Abraham, and Isaac, and Jacob, and all the prophets, in the kingdom of God, and you yourselves thrust out. And they shall come from the east, and from the west, and from the north, and from the south, and shall sit down in the kingdom of God. And, behold, there are last which shall be first, and there are first which shall be last.

The same day there came certain of the Pharisees, saying unto him, "Get thee out, and depart hence: for Herod will kill thee." And he said unto them, "Go ye, and tell that fox, Behold, I cast out devils, and I do cures to-day and to-morrow, and the third day I shall be perfected. Nevertheless I must walk to-day, and to-morrow, and the day following: for it cannot be that a prophet perish out of Jerusalem. O Jerusalem, Jerusalem, which killest the prophets, and stonest them that are sent unto thee; how often would I have gathered thy children together, as a hen doth gather her brood under her wings, and ye would not! Behold, your house is left unto you desolate: and verily I say unto you, Ye shall not see me, until the time come when ye shall say, Blessed is he that cometh in the name of the Lord."

And it came to pass, as he went into the house of one of the chief Pharisees to eat bread on the sabbath day, that they watched him. And, behold, there was a certain man before him which had the dropsy. And Jesus answering spake unto the lawyers and Pharisees, saying, "Is it lawful to heal on the sabbath day?" And they held their peace. And he took him, and healed him, and let him go; and answered them, saying, "Which of you shall have an ass or an ox fallen into a pit, and will not straightway pull him out on the sabbath day?" And they could not answer him again to these things.

And he put forth a parable to those which were bidden, when he marked how they chose out the chief rooms; saying unto them, "When thou art bidden of any man to a wedding, sit not down in the highest room; lest a more honorable man than thou be bidden of him; and

HEALING OF THE MAN WITH THE DROPSY.

he that bade thee and him come and say to thee, Give this man place;
and thou begin with shame to take the lowest room. But when thou art
bidden, go and sit down in the lowest room; that when he that bade thee
cometh, he may say unto thee, Friend, go up higher: then shalt thou
have worship in the presence of them that sit at meat with thee. For whosoever exalteth himself shall be abased; and he that humbleth himself shall
be exalted." Then said he also to him that bade him, " When thou makest
a dinner or a supper, call not thy friends, nor thy brethren, neither thy
kinsmen, nor thy rich neighbors; lest they also bid thee again, and a
recompense be made thee. But when thou makest a feast, Of inviting the poor to feasts.
call the poor, the maimed, the lame, the blind: and thou shalt
be blessed; for they cannot recompense thee; for thou shalt be recom-
pensed at the resurrection of the just."

And when one of them that sat at meat with him heard these things, he
said unto him, " Blessed is he that shall eat bread in the kingdom of God."
Then said he unto him, " A certain man made a great supper, and bade
many: and sent his servant at supper-time to say to them that were bidden,
Come; for all things are now ready. And they all with one consent be-
gan to make excuse. The first said unto him, I have bought a The parable of the great supper
piece of ground, and I must needs go and see it: I pray thee
have me excused. And another said, I have bought five yoke of oxen,
and I go to prove them: I pray thee have me excused. And another said,
I have married a wife, and therefore I cannot come. So that servant
came, and showed his lord these things. Then the master of the house
being angry said to his servant, Go out quickly into the streets and lanes
of the city, and bring in hither the poor, and the maimed, and the halt, and
the blind. And the servant said, Lord, it is done as thou hast commanded,
and yet there is room. And the lord said unto the servant, Go out into the
highways and hedges, and compel them to come in, that my house may be

filled. For I say unto you,
That none of those men
which were bidden shall
taste of my supper."

And there went great
multitudes with him: and
he turned, and said unto
them, " If any Of the cost of following Christ
man come to
me, and hate not his fa-
ther, and mother, and wife,
and children, and brethren,

TOWER IN VINEYARD.

and sisters, yea, and his own life also, he cannot be my disciple. And whosoever doth not bear his cross, and come after me, cannot be my disciple. For which of you, intending to build a tower, sitteth not down first, and counteth the cost, whether he have sufficient to finish it? lest haply, after he hath laid the foundation, and is not able to finish it, all that behold it begin to mock him, saying, This man began to build, and was not able to finish.

"Or what king, going to make war against another king, sitteth not down first, and consulteth whether he be able with ten thousand to meet him that cometh against him with twenty thousand? or else, while the other is yet a great way off, he sendeth an ambassage, and desireth conditions of peace. So likewise, whosoever he be of you that forsaketh not all that he hath, he cannot be my disciple.

The king with ten thousand.

"Salt is good: but if the salt have lost his savor, wherewith shall it be seasoned? it is neither fit for the land, nor yet for the dunghill; but men cast it out. He that hath ears to hear, let him hear."

Of salt without savor.

CHAPTER XXVIII.

FIVE GREAT PARABLES.

HEN drew near unto him all the publicans and sinners for to hear him. And the Pharisees and scribes murmured, saying, "This man receiveth sinners, and eateth with them." And he spake this parable unto them, saying, "What man of you, having an hundred sheep, if he lose one of them, doth not leave the ninety and nine in the wilderness, and go after that which is lost, until he find it? and when he hath found it, he layeth it on his shoulders, rejoicing. And when he cometh home, he calleth together his friends and neighbors, saying unto them,

The lost sheep.

Rejoice with me; for I have found my sheep which was lost. I say unto you, that likewise joy shall be in heaven over one sinner that repenteth, more than over ninety and nine just persons, which need no repentance.

"Either what woman having ten pieces of silver, if she lose one piece, doth not light a candle, and sweep the house, and seek diligently till she

The lost piece of silver.

find it? and when she hath found it, she calleth her friends and her neighbors together, saying, Rejoice with me; for I have found the piece which I had lost. Likewise, I say unto you, there is joy in the presence of the angels of God over one sinner that repenteth."

And he said, "A certain man had two sons: and the younger of them said to his father, Father, give me the portion of goods that falleth to me. And he divided unto them his living. And not many days after the younger son gathered all together, and took his journey into a far country, and there wasted his substance with riotous living. And when he had spent all, there arose a mighty famine in that land; and he began to be in want. And he went and joined himself to a citizen of that country; and he sent him into his fields to feed swine. And he would fain have filled his belly with the husks that the swine did eat: and no man gave unto him. And when he came to himself, he said, How many hired servants of my father's have bread enough and to spare, and I perish with hunger! I will arise and go to my father, and will say unto

DEPARTURE OF THE PRODIGAL SON 167

RETURN OF THE PRODIGAL SON.

him, Father, I have sinned against heaven, and before thee, and am no
more worthy to be called thy son: make me as one of thy
hired servants. And he arose, and came to his father. But *The prodigal son.*
when he was yet a great way off, his father saw him, and had compassion, and ran, and fell on his neck, and kissed him. And the son
said unto him, Father, I have sinned against heaven, and in thy sight,
and am no more worthy to be called thy son. But the father said to his
servants, Bring forth the best robe, and put it on him; and put a ring
on his hand, and shoes on his feet: and bring hither the fatted calf, and
kill it; and let us eat, and be merry: for this my son was dead, and is
alive again; he was lost, and is found. And they began to be merry.
Now his elder son was in the field: and as he came and drew nigh to
the house, he heard music and dancing. And he called one of the servants, and asked what these things meant. And he said unto him, Thy
brother is come; and thy father hath killed the fatted calf, because he hath
received him safe and sound. And he was angry, and would not go in:
therefore came his father out, and entreated him. And he answering said
to his father, Lo, these many years do I serve thee, neither transgressed I
at any time thy commandment: and yet thou never gavest me a kid, that
I might make merry with my friends: but as soon as this thy son was
come, which hath devoured thy living with harlots, thou hast killed for him
the fatted calf. And he said unto him, Son, thou art ever with me, and
all that I have is thine. It was meet that we should make merry, and be
glad: for this thy brother was dead, and is alive again; and was lost, and
is found."

And he said also unto his disciples, "There was a certain rich man,
which had a steward; and the same was accused unto him that he had
wasted his goods. And he called him, and said unto him, How is it that I
hear this of thee? give an account of thy stewardship; for thou *The unjust steward.*
mayest be no longer steward. Then the steward said within
himself, What shall I do? for my lord taketh away from me the stewardship: I cannot dig; to beg I am ashamed. I am resolved what to do, that,
when I am put out of the stewardship, they may receive me into their
houses. So he called every one of his lord's debtors unto him, and said
unto the first, How much owest thou unto my lord? And he said, An
hundred measures of oil. And he said unto him, Take thy bill, and sit
down quickly, and write fifty. Then said he to another, And how much
owest thou? And he said, An hundred measures of wheat. And he
said unto him, Take thy bill, and write fourscore. And the lord com-
mended the unjust steward, because he had done wisely: for the children
of this world are in their generation wiser than the children of light. And
I say unto you, Make to yourselves friends of the mammon of unrighteous-
v

ness; that, when ye fail, they may receive you into everlasting habitations. He that is faithful in that which is least is faithful also in much: and he that is unjust in the least is unjust also in much. If therefore ye have not been faithful in the unrighteous mammon, who will commit to your trust the true riches? And if ye have not been faithful in that which is another man's, who shall give you that which is your own? No servant can serve two masters: for either he will hate the one, and love the other; or else he will hold to the one, and despise the other. Ye cannot serve God and mammon."

And the Pharisees also, who were covetous, heard all these things: and they derided him. And he said unto them, "Ye are they which justify yourselves before men; but God knoweth your hearts: for that which is highly esteemed among men is abomination in the sight of God. The law and the prophets were until John: since that time the kingdom of God is preached, and every man presseth into it. And it is easier for heaven and earth to pass, than one tittle of the law to fail. Whosoever putteth away his wife, and marrieth another, committeth adultery: and whosoever marrieth her that is put away from her husband committeth adultery.

"There was a certain rich man, which was clothed in purple and fine linen, and fared sumptuously every day: and there was a certain beggar named Lazarus, which was laid at his gate, full of sores, and desiring to be fed with the crumbs which fell from the rich man's table: moreover the dogs came and licked his sores. And it came to pass, that the beggar died, and was carried by the angels into Abraham's bosom: the rich man also died, and was buried; and in hell he lift up his eyes, being in torments, and seeth Abraham afar off, and Lazarus in his bosom. And he cried and said, Father Abraham, have mercy on me, and send Lazarus, that he may dip the tip of his finger in water, and cool my tongue; for I am tormented in this flame. But Abraham said, Son, remember that thou in thy lifetime receivedst thy good things, and likewise Lazarus evil things: but now he is comforted, and thou art tormented. And beside all this, between us and you there is a great gulf fixed: so that they which would pass from hence to you cannot; neither can they pass to us, that would come from thence. Then he said, I pray thee therefore, father, that thou wouldest send him to my father's house: for I have five brethren; that he may testify unto them, lest they also come into this place of torment. Abraham saith unto him, They have Moses and the prophets; let them hear them. And he said, Nay, father Abraham: but if one went unto them from the dead, they will repent. And he said unto him, If they hear not Moses and the prophets, neither will they be persuaded, though one rose from the dead."

Then said he unto the disciples, "It is impossible but that offenses will

Of offenses. come: but woe unto him through whom they come! it were better for him that a millstone were hanged about his neck, and he cast into the sea, than that he should offend one of these little ones. Take heed to yourselves: if thy brother trespass against thee, rebuke him; and if he repent, forgive him. And if he trespass against thee seven times in a day, and seven times in a day turn again to thee, saying, I repent; thou shalt forgive him."

And the apostles said unto the Lord, "Increase our faith." And the

Of faith. Lord said, "If ye had faith as a grain of mustard-seed, ye might say unto this sycamine-tree, Be thou plucked up by the root, and be thou planted in the sea: and it should obey you. But which of you, having a servant plowing or feeding cattle, will say unto him by and by, when he is come from the field, Go and sit down to

Of our unprofitableness to God. meat? and will not rather say unto him, Make ready wherewith I may sup, and gird thyself, and serve me, till I have eaten and drunken: and afterward thou shalt eat and drink? doth he thank that servant because he did the things that were commanded him? I trow not. So likewise ye, when ye shall have done all those things which are commanded you, say, We are unprofitable servants: we have done that which was our duty to do."

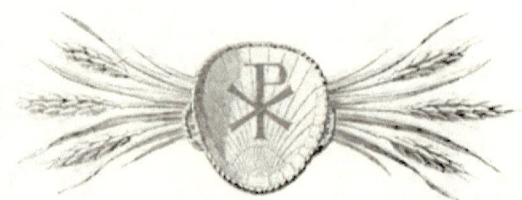

CHAPTER XXIX.

THE RAISING OF LAZARUS FROM THE DEAD.

OW a certain man was sick, named Lazarus, of Bethany, the town of Mary and her sister Martha. (It was that Mary which anointed the Lord with ointment, and wiped his feet with her hair, whose brother Lazarus was sick.) Therefore his sisters sent unto him, saying, "Lord, behold, he whom thou lovest is sick."

The sickness and death of Lazarus

When Jesus heard that, he said, "This sickness is not unto death, but for the glory of God, that the Son of God might be glorified thereby."

Now Jesus loved Martha, and her sister, and Lazarus. When he had heard therefore that he was sick, he abode two days still in the same place where he was. Then after that saith he to his disciples, "Let us go into Judæa again." His disciples say unto him, "Master, the Jews of late sought to stone thee; and goest thou thither again?" Jesus answered, "Are there not twelve hours in the day? If any man walk in the day he stumbleth not, because he seeth the light of this world. But if a man walk in the night, he stumbleth, because there is no light in him." These things said he: and after that he saith unto them, "Our friend Lazarus sleepeth; but I go, that I may awake him out of sleep." Then said his disciples, "Lord, if he sleep, he shall do well." Howbeit Jesus spake of his death: but they thought that he had spoken of taking of rest in sleep. Then said Jesus unto them plainly, "Lazarus is dead. And I am glad for your sakes that I was not there, to the intent ye may believe; nevertheless let us go unto him." Then said Thomas, which is called Didymus, unto his fellow-disciples, "Let us also go, that we may die with him."

Then when Jesus came, he found that he had lain in the grave four days already. Now Bethany was nigh unto Jerusalem, about fifteen furlongs off: and many of the Jews came to Martha and Mary,

The coming of Jesus.

to comfort them concerning their brother. Then Martha, as soon as she heard that Jesus was coming, went and met him: but Mary sat still in the house. Then said Martha unto Jesus, "Lord, if thou hadst been here, my brother had not died. But I know, that even now, whatsoever thou wilt ask of God, God will give it thee." Jesus saith unto her, "Thy brother shall rise again." Martha saith unto him, "I know that he shall rise again in the resurrection at the last day." Jesus said unto her, "I am the resurrection, and the life: he that believeth in me, though he were dead, yet shall he live: and whosoever liveth and believeth in me shall never die. Believest thou this?" She saith unto him, "Yea, Lord: I believe that thou art the Christ, the Son of God, which should come into the world." And when she had so said, she went her way, and called Mary her sister secretly, saying, "The Master is come, and calleth for thee." As soon as she heard that, she arose quickly, and came unto him. Now Jesus was not yet come into the town, but was in that place where Martha met him. The Jews then which were with her in the house, and comforted her, when they saw Mary, that she rose up hastily and went out, followed her, saying, "She goeth unto the grave to weep there." Then when Mary was come where Jesus was, and saw him, she fell down at his feet, saying unto him, "Lord, if thou hadst been here, my brother had not died." When Jesus therefore saw her weeping, and the Jews also weeping which came with her, he groaned in the spirit, and was troubled, and said, "Where have ye laid him?" They said unto him, "Lord, come and see." Jesus wept. Then said the Jews, "Behold how he loved him!" And some of them said, "Could not this man, which opened the eyes of the blind, have caused that even this man should not have died?" Jesus therefore again groaning in himself cometh to the grave. It was a cave, and a stone lay upon it. Jesus said, "Take ye away the stone." Martha, the sister of him that was

The raising of Lazarus. dead, saith unto him, "Lord, by this time he stinketh: for he hath been dead four days." Jesus saith unto her, "Said I not unto thee, that, if thou wouldest believe, thou shouldest see the glory of God?" Then they took away the stone from the place where the dead was laid. And Jesus lifted up his eyes and said, "Father, I thank thee that thou hast heard me. And I knew that thou hearest me always: but because of the people which stand by I said it, that they may believe that thou hast sent me." And when he thus had spoken, he cried with a loud voice, "Lazarus, come forth." And he that was dead came forth, bound hand and foot with graveclothes: and his face was bound about with a napkin. Jesus saith unto them, "Loose him, and let him go."

Then many of the Jews which came to Mary, and had seen the things which Jesus did, believed on him. But some of them went their ways to the Pharisees, and told them what things Jesus had done. Then gathered the chief priests and the Pharisees a council, and said, "What do we? for

The anger of the Sanhedrin. this man doeth many miracles. If we let him thus alone, all men will believe on him: and the Romans shall come and take away both our place and nation." And one of them, named Caiaphas,

being the high-priest that same year, said unto them, " Ye know nothing at all, nor consider that it is expedient for us, that one man should die for the people, and that the whole nation perish not." And this spake he not of himself: but being high-priest that year, he prophesied that Jesus should die for that nation ; and not for that nation only, but that also he should gather together in one the children of God that were scattered abroad. Then from that day forth they took counsel together for to put him to death. Jesus therefore walked no more openly among the Jews ; but went thence unto a country near to the wilderness, into a city called Ephraim, and there continued with his disciples.

CHAPTER XXX

FROM THE HEALING OF TEN LEPERS TO THE PARABLE OF THE LABORERS IN THE VINEYARD.

AND as he entered into a certain village, there met him ten men that were lepers, which stood afar off: and they lifted up their voices, and said, "Jesus, Master, have mercy on us." And when he saw them, he said unto them, "Go show yourselves unto the priests." And it came to pass, that, as they went, they were cleansed. And one of them, when he saw that he was healed, turned back, and with a loud voice glorified God, and fell down on his face at his feet, giving him thanks: and he was a Samaritan. And Jesus answering said, "Were there not ten cleansed? but where are the nine? there are not found that returned to give glory to God, save this stranger." And he said unto him, "Arise, go thy way: thy faith hath made thee whole."

The healing of ten lepers.

And when he was demanded of the Pharisees, when the kingdom of God should come, he answered them and said, "The kingdom of God cometh not with observation: neither shall they say, Lo here! or, Lo there! for, behold, the kingdom of God is within you."

And he said unto the disciples, "The days will come, when ye shall desire to see one of the days of the Son of man, and ye shall not see it. And they shall say to you, See here; or, See there: go not after them, nor follow them. For as the lightning, that lighteneth out of the one part under heaven, shineth unto the other part under heaven; so shall also the Son of man be in his day. But first must he suffer many things, and be rejected of the generation. And as it was in the days of Noah, so shall it be also in the days of the Son of man. They did eat, they drank, they married wives, they were given in marriage, until the day that Noah entered into the ark, and the flood came, and destroyed them all. Likewise also as it was in the days of Lot; they did eat, they drank, they bought, they sold, they planted, they builded; but the same day that Lot went out of Sodom it rained fire and brimstone from heaven, and destroyed them all. Even thus shall it be in the

The kingdom of God.

day when the Son of man is revealed. In that day, he which shall be upon the house-top, and his stuff in the house, let him not come down to take it away: and he that is in the field, let him likewise not return back. Remember Lot's wife. Whosoever shall seek to save his life shall lose it: and whosoever shall lose his life shall preserve it. I tell you, in that night there shall be two men in one bed: the one shall be taken, and the other shall be left. Two women shall be grinding together; the one shall be taken, and the other left. Two men shall be in the field: the one shall be taken,

ORIENTAL HOUSE-TOP.

and the other left." And they answered and said unto him, "Where, Lord?" And he said unto them, "Wheresoever the body is, thither will the eagles be gathered together."

WOMEN GRINDING AT A MILL.

And he spake a parable unto them to this end, that men ought always to pray, and not to faint; saying, "There was in the city a judge, which feared not God, neither regarded man: and there was a widow in that city; and she came unto him, saying, Avenge me of mine adversary. And

The unjust judge.

he would not for a while: but afterward he said within himself, Though I fear not God, nor regard man; yet because this widow troubleth me, I will avenge her, lest by her continual coming she weary me." And the Lord said, "Hear what the unjust judge saith. And shall not God avenge his own elect, which cry day and night unto him, though he bear long with them? I tell you that he will avenge them speedily. Nevertheless when the Son of man cometh, shall he find faith on the earth?"

And he spake this parable unto certain which trusted in themselves that they were righteous, and despised others: "Two men went up into the temple to pray; the one a Pharisee, and the other a publican. The Pharisee stood and prayed thus with himself, God, I thank thee, that I am not as other men are, extortioners, unjust, adulterers, or even as this publican. I fast twice in the week, I give tithes of all that I possess. And the publican, standing afar off, would not lift up so much as his eyes unto heaven, but smote upon his breast, saying, God be merciful to me a sinner. I tell you, this man went down to his house justified rather than the other: for every one that exalteth himself shall be abased; and he that humbleth himself shall be exalted."

The Pharisees also came unto him, tempting him, and saying unto him, "Is it lawful for a man to put away his wife for every cause?" And he answered and said unto them, "Have ye not read, that he which made them at the beginning made them male and female, and said, For this cause shall a man leave father and mother, and shall cleave to his wife: and they twain shall be one flesh? wherefore they are no more twain, but one flesh. What therefore God hath joined together, let not man put asunder." They say unto him, "Why did Moses then command to give a writing of divorcement, and to put her away?" He saith unto them, "Moses, because of the hardness of your hearts, suffered you to put away your wives: but from the beginning it was not so. And I say unto you, Whosoever shall put away his wife, except it be for fornication, and shall marry another, committeth adultery: and whoso marrieth her which is put away doth commit adultery." His disciples say unto him, "If the case of the man be so with his wife, it is not good to marry." But he said unto them, "All men cannot receive this saying, save they to whom it is given. For there are some eunuchs, which were so born from their mother's womb: and there are some eunuchs, which were made eunuchs of men: and there be eunuchs, which have made themselves eunuchs for the kingdom of heaven's sake. He that is able to receive it, let him receive it."

Then were there brought unto him little children, that he should put his hands on them, and pray: and the disciples rebuked them. But Jesus said, "Suffer little children, and forbid them not, to come unto me: for of such is the kingdom of heaven. Verily I say unto you, Whosoever shall not receive the kingdom of God as a little child, he shall

not enter therein." And he took them up in his arms, put his hands upon them, and blessed them.

And when he was gone forth into the way, there came a certain ruler running, and kneeled to him, and asked him, "Good Master, what shall I do that I may inherit eternal life?" And Jesus said unto him, "Why callest thou me good? there is none good but one, that is, God. But if thou wilt enter into life, keep the commandments." He saith unto him, "Which?" Jesus said, "Thou shalt do no murder, Thou shalt not commit adultery, Thou shalt not steal, Thou shalt not bear false witness, Honor thy father and thy mother: and, Thou shalt love thy neighbor as thyself." The young man saith unto him, "All these things have I kept from my youth up: what lack I yet?" Then Jesus beholding him loved him, and said unto him, "One thing thou lackest: go thy way, sell whatsoever thou hast, and give to the poor, and thou shalt have treasure in heaven: and come, take up the cross, and follow me." And he was sad at that saying, and went away grieved: for he had great possessions.

A young ruler inquires of Jesus.

And when Jesus saw that he was very sorrowful, he saith unto his disciples, "How hardly shall they that have riches enter into the kingdom of God!" And the disciples were astonished at his words. But Jesus answereth again, and saith unto them, "Children, how hard is it for them that trust in riches to enter into the kingdom of God! It is easier for a camel to go through the eye of a needle, than for a rich man to enter into the kingdom of God." And they were astonished out of measure, saying among themselves, "Who then can be saved?" And Jesus looking upon them saith, "With men it is impossible, but not with God: for with God all things are possible." Then

The danger of riches.

CAMEL PASSING THROUGH "NEEDLE's EYE."

answered Peter and said unto him, "Behold, we have forsaken all, and followed thee: what shall we have therefore?" And Jesus said unto them, "Verily I say unto you, That ye which have followed me, in the regeneration, when the Son of man shall sit in the throne of his glory, ye also shall sit upon twelve thrones, judging the twelve tribes

The reward of those that forsake all.

of Israel. There is no man that hath left house, or brethren, or sisters, or father, or mother, or wife, or children, or lands, for my sake, and the gospel's, but he shall receive an hundred-fold now in this time, houses, and brethren, and sisters, and mothers, and children, and lands, with persecutions; and in the world to come eternal life. But many that are first shall be last; and the last first. For the kingdom of heaven is like unto a man

The laborers in the vineyard. that is an householder, which went out early in the morning to hire laborers into his vineyard. And when he had agreed with the laborers for a penny a day, he sent them into his vineyard. And he went out about the third hour, and saw others standing idle in the market-place, and said unto them, Go ye also into the vineyard, and whatsoever is right I will give you. And they went their way. Again he went out about the sixth and ninth hour, and did likewise. And about the eleventh hour he went out, and found others standing idle, and saith unto them, Why stand ye here all the day idle? They say unto him, Because no man hath hired us. He saith unto them, Go ye also into the vineyard; and whatsoever is right, that shall ye receive. So when even was come,

the lord of the vineyard saith unto his steward, Call the laborers, and give them their hire, beginning from the last unto the first. And when they came that were hired about the eleventh hour, they received every man a penny. But when the first came, they supposed that they should have received more:

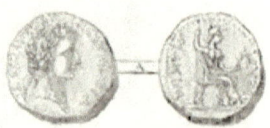

SILVER PENNY; TIME OF CÆSAR.

and they likewise received every man a penny. And when they had received it, they murmured against the goodman of the house, saying, These last have wrought but one hour, and thou hast made them equal unto us, which have borne the burden and heat of the day. But he answered one of them, and said, Friend, I do thee no wrong: didst not thou agree with me for a penny? Take that thine is, and go thy way: I will give unto this last, even as unto thee. Is it not lawful for me to do what I will with mine own? Is thine eye evil, because I am good? So the last shall be first, and the first last: for many be called, but few chosen."

CHAPTER XXXI.

JOURNEYING TOWARD JERUSALEM.

ND they were in the way going up to Jerusalem; and Jesus went before them; and they were amazed; and as they followed, they were afraid. And he took again the twelve, and began to tell them what things should happen unto him, saying, "Behold, we go up to Jerusalem, and all things that are written by the prophets concerning the Son of man shall be accomplished. For he shall be delivered unto the chief priests and unto the scribes, and they shall condemn him to death, and shall deliver him to the Gentiles to mock, and to scourge, and to crucify him: and the third day he shall rise again." And they understood none of these things: and this saying was hid from them, neither knew they the things which were spoken.

Christ foretelleth his death.

Then came to him the mother of Zebedee's children with her sons, worshiping him, and desiring a certain thing of him. And he said unto her, "What wilt thou?" She saith unto him, "Grant that these my two sons may sit, the one on thy right hand, and the other on the left, in thy kingdom." But Jesus answered and said, "Ye know not what ye ask. Are ye able to drink of the cup that I shall drink of, and to be baptized with the baptism that I am baptized with?" They say unto him, "We are able." And he saith unto them, "Ye shall drink indeed of my cup, and be baptized with the baptism that I am baptized with: but to sit on my right hand, and on my left, is not mine to give, but it shall be given to them for whom it is prepared of my Father." And when the ten heard it, they were moved with indignation against the two brethren. But Jesus called them unto him, and said, "Ye know that the princes of the Gentiles exercise dominion over them, and they that are great exercise authority upon them. But it shall not be so among you: but whosoever will be great among you, let him be your minister; and whosoever will be chief among you, let him be your servant: even as the Son of man came not to be ministered unto, but to minister, and to give his life a ransom for many."

The mother of Zebedee's children preferreth an ambitious request.

And they came to Jericho: and as he went out of Jericho with his disciples and a great number of people, blind Bartimeus, the son of Timeus, sat by the highway-side begging. And hearing the multitude pass by, he asked what it meant. And they told him, that Jesus of Nazareth passeth by. And he began to cry out, and say, "Jesus, thou son of David, have mercy on me." And many charged him that he should hold his peace: but he cried the more a great deal, "Thou son of David, have mercy on me." And Jesus stood still, and commanded him to be called. And they call the blind man, saying unto him, "Be of good comfort, rise; he calleth thee." And he, casting away his garment, rose, and came to Jesus. And Jesus answered and said unto him, "What wilt thou that I should do unto thee?" The blind man said unto him, "Lord, that I might receive my sight." So Jesus had compassion, and said unto him, "Receive thy sight: thy faith hath saved thee." And immediately he received his sight, and followed him, glorifying God: and all the people, when they saw it, gave praise unto God. *The healing of blind Bartimeus.*

And, behold, there was a man named Zaccheus, which was the chief among the publicans, and he was rich. And he sought to see Jesus who he was; and could not for the press, because he was little of stature. And he ran before, and climbed up into a sycamore-tree to see him: for he was to pass that way. And when Jesus came to the place, he looked up, and saw him, and said unto him, "Zaccheus, make haste, and come down; for to-day I must abide at thy house." And he made haste, and came down, and received him joyfully. And when they saw it, they all murmured, saying, "That he was gone to be guest with a man that is a sinner." And Zaccheus stood, and said unto the Lord: "Behold, Lord, the half of my goods I give to the poor; and if I have taken anything from any man by false accusation, I restore him fourfold." And Jesus said unto him, "This day is salvation come to this house, forsomuch as he also is a son of Abraham. For the Son of man is come to seek and to save that which was lost." *Zaccheus the publican.*

And as they heard these things, he added and spake a parable, because he was nigh to Jerusalem, and because they thought that the kingdom of God should immediately appear. He said therefore, "A certain nobleman went into a far country to receive for himself a kingdom, and to return. And he called his ten servants, and delivered them ten pounds, and said unto them, Occupy till I come. But his citizens hated him, and sent a message after him, saying, We will not have this man to reign over us. And it came to pass, that when he was returned, having received the kingdom, then he commanded these servants to be called unto him, to whom he had given the money, that he might know how much every man had gained by trading. Then came the first, saying, Lord, thy pound *The parable of the pounds.*

hath gained ten pounds. And he said unto him, Well, thou good servant: because thou hast been faithful in a very little, have thou authority over ten cities. And the second came, saying, Lord, thy pound hath gained five pounds. And he said likewise to him, Be thou also over five cities. And another came, saying, Lord, behold, here is thy pound, which I have kept laid up in a napkin: for I feared thee, because thou art an austere man: thou takest up that thou layedst not down, and reapest that thou didst not sow. And he saith unto him, Out of thine own mouth will I judge thee, thou wicked servant. Thou knewest that I was an austere man, taking up that I laid not down, and reaping that I did not sow: wherefore then gavest not thou my money into the bank, that at my coming I might have required mine own with usury? And he said unto them that stood by, Take from him the pound, and give it to him that hath ten pounds. And they said unto him, Lord, he hath ten pounds. (For I say unto you, That unto every one which hath shall be given; and from him that hath not, even that he hath shall be taken away from him.) But those mine enemies, which would not that I should reign over them, bring hither, and slay them before me." And when he had thus spoken, he went before, ascending up to Jerusalem.

And the Jews' passover was nigh at hand: and many went out of the country up to Jerusalem before the passover, to purify themselves. Then ~The Jews seek him at the feast.~ sought they for Jesus, and spake among themselves, as they stood in the temple, "What think ye, that he will not come to the feast?" Now both the chief priests and the Pharisees had given a commandment, that, if any man knew where he were, he should show it, that they might take him.

Then Jesus six days before the passover came to Bethany, where Lazarus was which had been dead, whom he raised from the dead.

Now when Jesus was in Bethany, in the house of Simon the leper, there they made him a supper; and Martha served: but Lazarus was one of them that sat at the table with him. Then took Mary a pound of ointment ~The alabaster box of ointment.~ of spikenard, very costly, and anointed the feet of Jesus, and wiped his feet with her hair: and the house was filled with the odor of the ointment. But when his disciples saw it, they had indignation. Then saith one of his disciples, Judas Iscariot, Simon's son, which should betray him, "Why was not this ointment sold for three hundred pence, and given to the poor?" This he said, not that he cared for the poor; but because he was a thief, and had the bag, and bare what was put therein. Then said Jesus, "Let her alone: against the day of my burying hath she kept this. For the poor always ye have with you; but me ye have not always. She hath done what she could: she is come aforehand to anoint my body to the burying. Verily I say unto you, Wheresoever this gospel shall be preached throughout the whole world, this also that she hath done shall be spoken of for a memorial of her."

Much people of the Jews therefore knew that he was there: and they came not for Jesus' sake only, but that they might see Lazarus also, whom he had raised from the dead. But the chief priests consulted that they might put Lazarus also to death; because that by reason of him many of the Jews went away, and believed on Jesus.

CHAPTER XXXII.

CHRIST'S TRIUMPHAL ENTRY, AND THE EVENTS WHICH FOLLOWED.

 N the next day much people that were come to the feast, when they heard that Jesus was coming to Jerusalem, took branches of palm-trees, and went forth to meet him. And it came to pass, when he was come nigh to Bethphage and Bethany, at the mount called the mount of Olives, he sent two of his disciples, saying, "Go ye into the village over against you; in the which at your entering ye shall find a colt tied, whereon yet never man sat: loose him, and bring him hither. And if any man ask you, Why do ye loose him? thus shall ye say unto him, Because the Lord hath need of him." And they that were sent went their way, and found even as he had said unto them. And as they were loosing the colt, the owners thereof said unto them, "Why loose ye the colt?" And they said, "The Lord hath need of him." And they brought him to Jesus: and they cast their garments upon the colt, and they set Jesus thereon; as it is written, "Fear not, daughter of Sion: behold, thy King cometh, sitting on an ass's colt." These things understood not his disciples at the first: but when Jesus was glorified, then remembered they that these things were written of him, and that they had done these things unto him. The people therefore that was with him when he called Lazarus out of his grave, and raised him from the dead, bare record. For this cause the people also met him, for that they heard that he had done this miracle.

Christ's triumphal entry into Jerusalem. And many spread their garments in the way: and others cut down branches off the trees, and strewed them in the way. And when he was come nigh, even now at the descent of the mount of Olives, the whole multitude of the disciples began to rejoice and praise God with a loud voice for all the mighty works that they had seen; and cried, "Hosanna: Blessed is the King of Israel that cometh in the name of the Lord. Blessed be the kingdom of our father David, that cometh in the name of the Lord: Hosanna in the highest." And some of the Pharisees from among the multitude said unto him, "Master, rebuke thy disciples." And he answered and said unto them, "I tell

THE SHE-ASS AND HER COLT.

you that, if these should hold their peace, the stones would immediately cry out."

And when he was come near, he beheld the city, and wept over it, say-

He weeps over Jerusalem. ing, "If thou hadst known, even thou, at least in this thy day, the things which belong unto thy peace! but now they are hid from thine eyes. For the days shall come upon thee, that thine enemies shall cast a trench about thee, and compass thee round, and keep thee in on every side, and shall lay thee even with the ground, and thy children within thee; and they shall not leave in thee one stone upon another; because thou knewest not the time of thy visitation."

And when he was come into Jerusalem, all the city was moved, saying, "Who is this?" And the multitude said, "This is Jesus the prophet of Nazareth of Galilee." And the blind and the lame came to him in the

The chief priests are displeased. temple; and he healed them. And when the chief priests and scribes saw the wonderful things that he did, and the children crying in the temple, and saying, "Hosanna to the son of David"; they were sore displeased, and said unto him, "Hearest thou what these say?" And Jesus saith unto them, "Yea: have ye never read, Out of the mouth of babes and sucklings thou hast perfected praise?" And he left them and went out of the city to Bethany and lodged there.

And on the morrow, when they were come from Bethany, he was hun-

The fig-tree is cursed. gry: and seeing a fig-tree afar off having leaves, he came, if haply he might find anything thereon: and when he came to it, he found nothing but leaves; for the time of figs was not yet. And Jesus answered and said unto it, "No man eat fruit of thee hereafter forever." And his disciples heard it.

And they come to Jerusalem: and Jesus went into the temple, and began

The second cleansing of the temple to cast out them that sold and bought in the temple, and over- threw the tables of the money-changers, and the seats of them that sold doves; and would not suffer that any man should carry any vessel through the temple. And he taught, saying unto them, "Is it not written, My house shall be called of all nations the house of prayer? but ye have made it a den of thieves." And he taught daily in the temple. But the chief priests and the scribes and the chief of the people sought to destroy him, and could not find what they might do: for all the people were very attentive to hear him. And when even was come, he went out of the city.

And in the morning, as they passed by, they saw the fig-tree dried up

The withered fig tree from the roots. And Peter calling to remembrance saith unto him, "Master, behold, the fig-tree which thou cursedst is with- ered away." And Jesus answering saith unto them, "Have faith in God. For verily I say unto you, That whosoever shall say unto this mountain,

Be thou removed, and be thou cast into the sea; and shall not doubt in his heart, but shall believe that those things which he saith shall come to pass; he shall have whatsoever he saith. Therefore I say unto you, What things soever ye desire, when ye pray, believe that ye receive them, and ye shall have them. And when ye stand praying, forgive, if ye have aught against any: that your Father also which is in heaven may forgive you your trespasses. But if ye do not forgive, neither will your Father which is in heaven forgive your trespasses.

TRIUMPHAL ENTRY INTO JERUSALEM.

CHAPTER XXXIII.

AND they come again to Jerusalem: as he taught the people in the temple, and preached the gospel, there came to him the chief priests, and the scribes, and the elders, and say unto him, "By what authority doest thou these things? and who gave thee this authority to do these things?"

And Jesus answered and said unto them, "I will also ask of you one question, and answer me, and I will tell you by what authority I do these things. The baptism of John, was it from heaven, or of men? answer me." And they reasoned with themselves, saying, "If we shall say, From heaven; he will say, Why then did ye not believe him? But if we shall say, Of men; they feared the people: for all men counted John, that he was a prophet indeed. And they answered and said unto Jesus, "We cannot tell." And Jesus answering saith unto them, "Neither do I tell you by what authority I do these things."

The Sanhedrim questions his authority.

And he began to speak unto them by parables. "A certain man had two sons; and he came to the first, and said, Son, go work to-day in my vineyard. He answered and said, I will not: but afterward he repented, and went. And he came to the second, and said likewise. And he answered and said, I go, sir: and went not. Whether of them twain did the will of his father?" They say unto him, "The first." Jesus saith unto them, "Verily I say unto you, That the publicans and the harlots go into the kingdom of God before you. For John came unto you in the way of righteousness, and ye believed him not: but the publicans and the harlots believed him: and ye, when ye had seen it, repented not afterward, that ye might believe him.

The parable of the two sons.

"Hear another parable: There was a certain householder, which planted a vineyard, and hedged it round about, and digged a wine-press in it, and built a tower, and let it out to husbandmen, and went into a far country. And at the season he sent a servant to the husbandmen, that they should give him of the fruit of the vineyard: but the husbandmen beat him, and sent him away empty. And again he sent another

The parable of the vineyard let out to husbandmen.

servant: and they beat him also, and entreated him shamefully, and sent him away empty. And again he sent a third: and they wounded him also, and cast him out. Having yet therefore one

WINE-PRESS IN ORIENTAL VINEYARD.

son, his well-beloved, he sent him also last unto them, saying, They will reverence my son, when they see him. But when the husbandmen saw him, they reasoned among themselves, saying, This is the heir: come, let us kill him, that the inheritance may be ours. So they cast him out of the vineyard, and killed him. What therefore shall the lord of the vineyard do unto them? he shall come and destroy these husbandmen, and shall give the vineyard to others." And when they heard it, they said, "God forbid." And he beheld them, and said, "What is this then that is written, The stone which the builders rejected, the same is become the head of the corner? this is the Lord's doing, and it is marvelous in our eyes! Therefore say I unto you, The kingdom of God shall be taken from you, and given to a nation bringing forth the fruits thereof. And whosoever shall fall on this stone shall be broken: but on whomsoever it shall fall, it will grind him to powder." And the chief priests and the scribes the same hour sought to lay hands on him; and they feared the people: for they perceived that he had spoken this parable against them.

And Jesus answered and spake unto them again by parables, and said, "The kingdom of heaven is like unto a certain king, which made a marriage for his son, and sent forth his servants to call them that were bidden to the wedding: and they would not come. Again, he sent forth other servants, saying, Tell them which are bidden, Behold, I have prepared my dinner: my oxen and my fatlings are killed, and all things are ready: come unto the marriage. But they made light of it, and went their ways, one to his farm, another to his merchandise: and the remnant took his servants, and entreated them spitefully, and slew them. But when the king heard thereof, he was wroth: and he sent forth his armies, and destroyed those murderers, and burned up their city. Then saith he to his servants, The wedding is ready, but they which were bidden were not worthy. Go ye therefore into the highways, and as many as ye shall find, bid to the marriage. So those servants went out into the highways, and gathered together all as many as they found, both bad and good: and the wedding was furnished with guests. And when the king came in to see the guests, he saw there a man which had not on a wedding garment: and he saith unto him, Friend, how camest thou in hither not having a wedding garment? And he was speechless. Then said the king to the servants, Bind him hand and foot, and take him away, and cast him into outer darkness; there shall be weeping and gnashing of teeth. For many are called, but few are chosen."

Then went the Pharisees, and took counsel how they might entangle him in his talk. And they sent out unto him their disciples with the Herodians, that they might take hold of his words, that so they might deliver him unto the power and authority of the governor. And they asked him, saying, "Master, we know that thou art true, and teachest the way of God in truth, neither carest thou for any man: for thou regardest not the person of men. Tell us therefore, What thinkest thou? Is it lawful to give tribute unto Cæsar, or not?" But Jesus perceived their wickedness, and said, "Why tempt ye me, ye hypocrites? show me the tribute money."

A question about tribute.

And they brought unto him a penny. And he saith unto them, "Whose is this image and superscription?" They say unto him, "Cæsar's." Then saith he unto them, "Render therefore unto Cæsar the things which are Cæsar's; and unto God the things that are God's." And they could not take hold of his words before the people: and they marveled at his answer, and held their peace, and left him, and went their way.

The same day came to him the Sadducees, which say that there is no resurrection, and asked him, saying, "Master, Moses said, If a man die, having no children, his brother shall marry his wife, and raise up seed unto his brother. Now there were with us seven brethren: and the first, when he had married a wife, deceased, and, having no issue, left his wife unto his brother: likewise the second also, and the third, unto the seventh. And last of all the woman died also. Therefore in the resurrection whose wife shall she be of the seven? for they all had her." Jesus answered and said unto them, "Ye do err, not knowing the scriptures, nor the power of God. The children of this world marry, and are given in marriage: but

Concerning marriage in heaven.

they which shall be accounted worthy to obtain that world, and the resurrection from the dead, neither marry, nor are given in marriage: neither can they die any more: for they are equal unto the angels; and are the children of God, being the children of the resurrection. And as touching the dead, that they rise: have ye not read in the book of Moses, how in the bush God spake unto him, saying, I am the God of Abraham, and the God of Isaac, and the God of Jacob? He is not the God of the dead, but the God of the living: ye therefore do greatly err." And when the multitude heard this, they were astonished at his doctrine.

But when the Pharisees had heard that he had put the Sadducees to silence, they were gathered together. Then one of them, which

A lawyer asks which is the first commandment of all.

was a lawyer, asked him a question, tempting him, and saying, "Master, which is the first commandment of all?" And Jesus answered him, "The first of all the commandments is, Hear, O Israel;

The Lord our God is one Lord: and thou shalt love the Lord thy God with all thy heart, and with all thy soul, and with all thy mind, and with all thy strength: this is the first commandment. And the second is like, namely this, Thou shalt love thy neighbor as thyself. On these two commandments hang all the law and the prophets." And the scribe said unto him, "Well, Master, thou hast said the truth: for there is one God; and there is none other but he: and to love him with all the heart, and with all the understanding, and with all the soul, and with all the strength, and to love his neighbor as himself, is more than all whole burnt-offerings and sacrifices." And when Jesus saw that he answered discreetly, he said unto him, "Thou art not far from the kingdom of God."

While the Pharisees were gathered together, Jesus asked them, saying, He asketh the Pharisees concerning Christ. "What think ye of Christ? whose son is he?" They say unto him, "The son of David." He saith unto them, "How then doth David in spirit call him Lord, saying, The LORD said unto my Lord, Sit thou on my right hand, till I make thine enemies thy footstool? If David then call him Lord, how is he his son?" And no man was able to answer him a word, neither durst any man from that day forth ask him any more questions. And the common people heard him gladly.

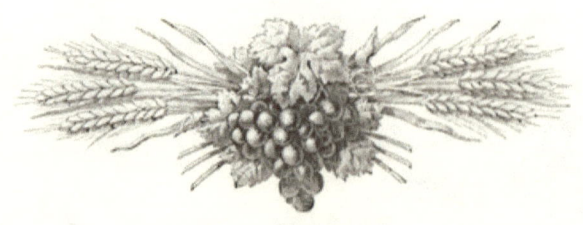

"THE SCRIBES AND PHARISEES SIT IN MOSES' SEAT"

CHAPTER XXXIV.

HEN spake Jesus to the multitude, and to his disciples, saying, "The scribes and the Pharisees sit in Moses' seat: all therefore whatsoever they bid you observe, that observe and do; but do not ye after their works: for they say, and do not. For they bind heavy burdens and grievous to be borne, and lay them on men's shoulders; but they themselves will not move them with one of their fingers. But all their works they do for to be seen of men: they make broad their phylac-

teries, and enlarge the borders of their garments, and love the uppermost rooms at
feasts, and the chief seats in the synagogues,
and greetings in the markets, and to be called
of men, Rabbi, Rabbi. But be not ye called

PHYLACTERIES: WORN ON THE ARM.

Rabbi: for one is your Master, even Christ; and all ye are brethren. And call no man your father upon the earth: for one is your Father, which is in heaven. Neither be ye called masters: for one is your Master, even

PHYLACTERIES, OR FRONTLETS: WORN ON FOREHEAD.

Christ. But he that is greatest among you shall be your servant. And whosoever shall exalt himself shall be abased; and he that shall humble himself shall be exalted. But woe unto you, scribes and Pharisees, hypo-crites! for ye shut up the kingdom of heaven against men: for ye neither go in yourselves, neither suffer ye them that are entering to go in. Woe unto you, scribes and Pharisees, hypocrites! for ye devour widows' houses, and

for a pretense make long prayer: therefore ye shall receive the greater damnation. Woe unto you, scribes and Pharisees, hypocrites! for ye compass sea and land to make one proselyte, and when he is made, ye make him twofold more the child of hell than yourselves. Woe unto

you, ye blind guides, which say, Whosoever shall swear by the temple, it is nothing; but whosoever shall swear by the gold of the temple, he is a debtor! Ye fools and blind: for whether is greater, the gold, or the temple that sanctifieth the gold? And, Whosoever shall swear by the altar, it is nothing; but whosoever sweareth by the gift that is upon it, he is guilty. Ye fools and blind: for whether is greater, the gift, or the altar that sanctifieth the gift? whoso therefore shall swear by the altar, sweareth by it, and by all things thereon. And whoso shall swear by the temple, sweareth by it, and by him that dwelleth therein. And he that shall swear by heaven, sweareth by the throne of God, and by him that sitteth thereon. Woe unto you, scribes and Pharisees, hypocrites! for ye pay tithe of mint and anise and cummin, and have omitted the weightier matters of the law, judgment, mercy, and faith: these ought ye to have done, and not to leave the other undone. Ye blind guides, which strain at a gnat, and swallow a camel. Woe unto you, scribes and Pharisees, hypocrites! for ye make clean the outside of the cup and of the platter, but within they are full of extortion and excess. Thou blind Pharisee, cleanse first that which is within the cup and platter, that the outside of them may be clean also. Woe unto you, scribes and Pharisees, hypocrites! for ye are like unto whited sepulchers, which indeed appear beautiful outward, but are within full of dead men's bones, and of all uncleanness. Even so ye also outwardly appear righteous unto men, but within ye are full of hypocrisy and iniquity. Woe unto you, scribes and Pharisees, hypocrites! because ye build the tombs of the prophets, and garnish the sepulchers of the righteous, and say, If we had been in the days of our fathers, we would not have been partakers with them in the blood of the prophets. Wherefore ye be witnesses unto yourselves, that ye are the children of them which killed the prophets. Fill ye up then the measure of your fathers. Ye serpents, ye generation of vipers, how can ye escape the damnation of hell? Wherefore, behold, I send unto you prophets, and wise men, and scribes: and some of them ye shall kill and crucify; and some of them shall ye scourge in your synagogues, and persecute them from city to city: that upon you may come all the righteous blood shed upon the earth, from the blood of righteous Abel unto the blood of Zacharias, son of Barachias, whom ye slew between the temple and the altar. Verily I say unto you, All these things shall come upon this generation. O Jerusalem, Jerusalem, thou that killest the prophets, and stonest them which are sent unto Lamentation over the fate of Jerusalem.
thee, how often would I have gathered thy children together, even as a hen gathereth her chickens under her wings, and ye would not! Behold, your house is left unto you desolate. For I say unto you, Ye shall not see me henceforth, till ye shall say, Blessed is he that cometh in the name of the Lord."

And Jesus sat over against the treasury, and beheld how the people cast money into the treasury: and many that were rich cast in much. And there came a certain poor widow, and she threw in two mites, 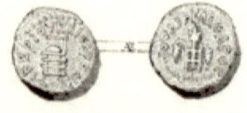 which make a farthing. And he called

The two mites of a poor widow.

unto him his disciples, and saith unto them, "Verily I say unto you, That this poor

LEPTON (MITE OF TIBERIUS.)

widow hath cast more in, than all they which have cast into the treasury: for all they did cast in of their abundance; but she of her want did cast in all that she had, even all her living."

And there were certain Greeks among them that came up to worship at the feast: the same came therefore to Philip, which was of Bethsaida of Galilee, and desired him, saying, Sir, we would see Jesus. Philip cometh and telleth Andrew: and again Andrew and Philip tell Jesus.

Certain Greeks seek to see Jesus.

And Jesus answered them, saying, "The hour is come, that the Son of man should be glorified. Verily, verily, I say unto you, Except a corn of wheat fall into the ground and die, it abideth alone: but if it die, it bringeth forth much fruit. He that loveth his life shall lose it; and he that hateth his life in this world shall keep it unto life eternal. If any man serve me, let him follow me; and where I am, there shall also my servant be: if any man serve me, him will my Father honor. Now is my soul troubled: and what shall I say? Father, save me from this hour: but for this cause came I unto this hour. Father, glorify thy name." Then came there a voice from heaven, saying, "I have both glorified it, and will glorify it again." The people therefore, that stood by, and heard it, said that it thundered: others said, "An angel spake to him." Jesus answered and said, "This voice came not because of me, but for your sakes. Now is the judgment of this world: now shall the prince of this world be cast out. And I, if I be lifted up from the earth, will draw all men unto me." This he said, signifying what death he should die. The people answered him, "We have heard out of the law that Christ abideth forever: and how sayest thou, The Son of man must be lifted up? who is this Son of man?" Then Jesus said unto them, "Yet a little while is the light with you. Walk while ye have the light, lest darkness come upon you: for he that walketh in darkness knoweth not whither he goeth. While ye have light, believe in the light, that ye may be the children of light."

But though he had done so many miracles before them, yet they believed not on him: that the saying of Isaiah the prophet might be fulfilled, which

Unbelief of the Jews.

he spake, "Lord, who hath believed our report? and to whom hath the arm of the Lord been revealed?" Therefore they could not believe, because that Isaiah said again, "He hath blinded their eyes, and hardened their heart; that they should not see with their eyes,

nor understand with their heart, and be converted, and I should heal them." These things said Isaiah, when he saw his glory, and spake of him. Nevertheless among the chief rulers also many believed on him; but because of the Pharisees they did not confess him, lest they should be put out of the synagogue: for they loved the praise of men more than the praise of God.

Jesus cried and said, " He that believeth on me, believeth not on me, but on him that sent me. And he that seeth me seeth him that sent me. I am come a light into the world, that whosoever believeth on me should not abide in darkness. And if any man hear my words, and believe not, I judge him not: for I came not to judge the world, but to save the world. He that rejecteth me, and receiveth not my words, hath one that judgeth him: the word that I have spoken, the same shall judge him in the last day. For I have not spoken of myself; but the Father which sent me, he gave me a commandment, what I should say, and what I should speak. And I know that his commandment is life everlasting: whatsoever I speak therefore, even as the Father said unto me, so I speak."

He that believes on Jesus believes on God.

JESUS FORETELLS THE DESTRUCTION OF THE TEMPLE.

CHAPTER XXXV.

THE DESTRUCTION OF JERUSALEM, AND THE LAST JUDGMENT.

ND as he went out of the temple, one of his disciples saith unto him, "Master, see what manner of stones and what buildings are here!" And Jesus answering said unto him, "Seest thou these great buildings? the days will come, in the which there shall not be left one stone upon another, that shall not be thrown down."

And as he sat upon the mount of Olives over against the temple, Peter and James and John and Andrew asked him privately, "Tell us, when shall these things be? and what shall be the sign of thy coming and of the end of the world?" And Jesus answering them began to say, *Prophecy concerning the destruction of Jerusalem.* "Take heed lest any man deceive you: for many shall come in my name, saying, I am Christ; and shall deceive many: and the time draweth near: go ye not therefore after them. But when ye shall hear of wars and commotions, be not terrified: for these things must first come to pass; but the end is not by and by." Then said he unto them, "Nation shall rise against nation, and kingdom against kingdom: and great earthquakes shall be in divers places, and famines, and pestilences; and fearful sights and great signs shall there be from heaven. These are the beginnings of sorrows. Then shall many be offended. But take heed to yourselves; for before all this they shall deliver you up to councils and into prisons, and in the synagogues ye shall be beaten, and ye shall be brought before kings and rulers for my name's sake. And it shall turn to you for a testimony. Settle it therefore in your hearts, not to meditate before what ye shall answer: for I will give you a mouth and wisdom, which all your adversaries shall not be able to gainsay nor resist. Now the brother shall betray the brother to death, and the father the son; and children shall rise up against their parents, and shall cause them to be put to death. And ye shall be hated of all men for my name's sake. But there shall not an hair of your head perish. In your patience possess ye your souls. And many false prophets shall rise, and shall deceive many. And because iniquity shall abound, the love of many shall wax cold. But

JESUS UPON THE MOUNT OF OLIVES

he that shall endure unto the end, the same shall be saved. And this gospel of the kingdom shall be preached in all the world for a witness unto all nations; and then shall the end come.

"When ye therefore shall see the abomination of desolation, spoken of by Daniel the prophet, stand in the holy place, (whoso readeth, let him understand:) then let them which be in Judæa flee into the mountains: let him which is on the house-top not come down to take anything out of his house: neither let him which is in the field return back to take his clothes. For these be the days of vengeance, that all things which are written may be fulfilled. And woe unto them that are with child, and to them that give suck in those days! But pray ye that your flight be not in the winter, neither on the sabbath day; for in those days shall be affliction, such as was not from the beginning of the creation which God created unto this time, neither shall be. And they shall fall by the edge of the sword, and shall be led away captive into all nations: and Jerusalem shall be trodden down of the Gentiles, until the times of the Gentiles be fulfilled. And except those days should be shortened, there should no flesh be saved: but for the elect's sake those days shall be shortened. Then if any man shall say unto you, Lo, here is Christ, or there; believe it not. For there shall arise false Christs, and false prophets, and shall show great signs and wonders: insomuch that, if it were possible, they shall deceive the very elect. Behold, I have told you before. Wherefore if they shall say unto you, Behold, he is in the desert: go not forth: Behold, he is in the secret chambers; believe it not. For as the lightning cometh out of the east, and shineth even unto the west; so shall also the coming of the Son of man be. For wheresoever the carcass is, there will the eagles be gathered together. Immediately after the tribulation of those days shall the sun be darkened, and the moon shall not give her light, and the stars shall fall from heaven. And there shall be upon the earth distress of nations, with perplexity; the sea and the waves roaring: men's hearts failing them for fear, and for looking after those things which are coming on the earth: for the powers of heaven shall be shaken. And then shall appear the sign of the Son of man in heaven: and then shall all the tribes of the earth mourn, and they shall see the Son of man coming in the clouds of heaven with power and great glory. And he shall send his angels with a great sound of a trumpet, and they shall gather together his elect from the four winds, from one end of heaven to the other. And when these things begin to come to pass, then look up, and lift up your heads; for your redemption draweth nigh.

"Now learn a parable of the fig-tree; When his branch is yet tender, and putteth forth leaves, ye know that summer is nigh: so likewise ye, when ye shall see all these things, know that the kingdom of God is near, even at the doors. Verily I say unto you, This generation shall not pass, till all these things be fulfilled. Heaven and earth shall pass away, but my words shall not pass away. But of that day and that hour knoweth no man, no, not the angels which are in heaven, neither the Son, but the Father. But as the days of Noah were, so shall also the coming of the Son of man be. For as in the days that were before the flood they were eating and drinking, marrying and giving in marriage, until the day that Noah entered into the ark, and knew not until the flood came, and took them all away; so shall also the coming of the Son of man be. Then shall two be in the field; the one shall be taken, and the other left. Two women shall be grinding at the mill: the one shall be taken, and the other left. And take heed to yourselves, lest at any time your hearts be overcharged with surfeiting, and drunkenness, and cares of this life, and so that day come upon you unawares. For as a snare shall it come on all them that dwell on the face of the whole earth. Watch therefore: for ye know *Christ cometh as* not what hour your Lord doth come. But know this, that if *a thief in the night.* the goodman of the house had known in what watch the thief would come, he would have watched, and would not have suffered his house to be broken up. Therefore be ye also ready: for in such an hour as ye think not the Son of man cometh. Who then is a faithful and wise *The faithful and* servant, whom his lord hath made ruler over his household, to *wise servant.* give them meat in due season? Blessed is that servant, whom his lord when he cometh shall find so doing. Verily I say unto you, That he shall make him ruler over all his goods. But and if that evil servant shall say in his heart, My lord delayeth his coming; and shall begin to smite his fellow-servants, and to eat and drink with the drunken; the lord of that servant shall come in a day when he looketh not for him, and in an hour that he is not aware of, and shall cut him asunder, and appoint him his portion with the hypocrites: there shall be weeping and gnashing of teeth. Watch ye therefore: for ye know not when the master of the house cometh, at even, or at midnight, or at the cock-crowing, or in the morning: lest coming suddenly he find you sleeping. And what I say unto you I say unto all, Watch.

"Then shall the kingdom of heaven be likened unto ten virgins, which took their lamps, and went forth to meet the bridegroom. And five of them were wise, and five were foolish. They that were foolish took their lamps, and took no oil with them: but the wise took oil in their vessels with their lamps. While the bridegroom tarried, they all slumbered and *Parable of the ten* slept. And at midnight there was a cry made, Behold, the *virgins.* bridegroom cometh; go ye out to meet him. Then all those virgins arose, and trimmed their lamps. And the foolish said unto the wise, Give us of your oil; for our lamps are gone out. But the wise answered, saying, Not so; lest there be not enough for us and you: but go ye rather to them that sell, and buy for yourselves. And while they went to buy, the bridegroom came; and they that were ready went in with him to the marriage: and the door was shut. Afterward came also the other virgins, saying, Lord, Lord, open to us. But he answered and said, Verily I say unto you, I know you not. Watch therefore, for ye know neither the day nor the hour wherein the Son of man cometh."

"For the kingdom of heaven is as a man traveling into a far country, who called his own servants, and delivered unto them his goods. And unto one

Parable of the talents

he gave five talents, to another two, and to another one; to every man according to his several ability; and straightway took his journey. Then he that had received the five talents went and traded with the same, and made them other five talents. And likewise he that had received two, he also gained other two. But he that had received one went and digged in the earth, and hid his lord's money. After a long time the lord of those servants cometh, and reckoneth with them. And so he that had received five talents came and brought other five talents, saying, Lord, thou deliveredst unto me five talents: behold, I have gained beside them five talents more. His lord said unto him, Well done, thou good and faithful servant: thou hast been faithful over a few things, I will make thee ruler over many things: enter thou into the joy of thy lord. He also that had received two talents came and said, Lord, thou deliveredst unto me two talents: behold, I have gained two other talents beside them. His lord said unto him, Well done, good and faithful servant: thou hast been faithful over a few things, I will make thee ruler over many things: enter thou into the joy of thy lord. Then he which had received the one talent came and said, Lord, I knew thee that thou art an hard man, reaping where thou hast not sown, and gathering where thou hast not strawed: and I was afraid, and went and hid thy talent in the earth: lo, there thou hast that is thine. His lord answered and said unto him, Thou wicked and slothful servant, thou knewest that I reap where I sowed not, and gather where I have not strawed: thou oughtest therefore to have put my money to the exchangers, and then at my coming I should have received mine own with usury. Take therefore the talent from him, and give it unto him which hath ten talents. For unto every one that hath shall be given, and he shall have abundance: but from him that hath not shall be taken away even that which he hath. And cast ye the unprofitable servant into outer darkness: there shall be weeping and gnashing of teeth.

"When the Son of man shall come in his glory, and all the holy angels with him, then shall he sit upon the throne of his glory: and before him

Of the last judgment

shall be gathered all nations: and he shall separate them one from another, as a shepherd divideth his sheep from the goats: and he shall set the sheep on his right hand, but the goats on the left.

THE FOOLISH VIRGINS.

Then shall the King say unto them on his right hand, Come, ye blessed of my Father, inherit the kingdom prepared for you from the foundation of the world: for I was anhungered, and ye gave me meat: I was thirsty, and ye gave me drink: I was a stranger, and ye took me in: naked, and ye clothed me: I was sick, and ye visited me: I was in prison, and ye came unto me. Then shall the righteous answer him, saying, Lord, when saw we thee anhungered, and fed thee? or thirsty, and gave thee drink? when saw we thee a stranger, and took thee in? or naked, and clothed thee? or when saw we thee sick, or in prison, and came unto thee? And the King shall answer and say unto them, Verily I say unto you, Inasmuch as ye have done it unto one of the least of these my brethren, ye have done it unto me. Then shall he say also unto them on the left hand, Depart from me, ye cursed, into everlasting fire, prepared for the devil and his angels: for I was anhungered, and ye gave me no meat: I was thirsty, and ye gave me no drink: I was a stranger, and ye took me not in: naked, and ye clothed me not: sick, and in prison, and ye visited me not. Then shall they also answer him, saying, Lord, when saw we thee anhungered, or athirst, or a stranger, or naked, or sick, or in prison, and did not minister unto thee? Then shall he answer them, saying, Verily I say unto you, Inasmuch as ye did it not to one of the least of these, ye did it not to me. And these shall go away into everlasting punishment: but the righteous into life eternal."

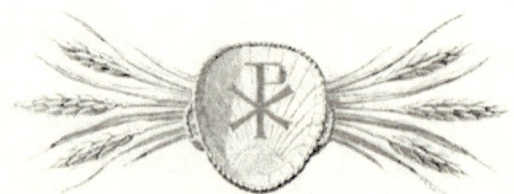

CHAPTER XXXVI.

THE LAST SUPPER.

AND it came to pass, when Jesus had finished all these sayings, he said unto his disciples, "Ye know that after two days is the feast of the passover, and the Son of man is betrayed to be crucified."

Then assembled together the chief priests, and the scribes, and the elders of the people, unto the palace of the high-priest, who was called Caiaphas, and consulted that they might take Jesus by subtilty, and kill him. But they said, "Not on the feast-day, lest there be an uproar among the people."

Then entered Satan into Judas surnamed Iscariot, being of the number of the twelve. And he went his way, and communed with the chief priests and captains, how he might betray him unto them. And he said unto them, "What will ye give me, and I will deliver him unto you?" And they covenanted with him for thirty pieces of silver. And he promised, and sought opportunity to betray him unto them in the absence of the multitude.

The treachery of Judas.

SILVER TETRADRACHM PAID JUDAS.

Now the first day of the feast of unleavened bread, when the passover must be killed, the disciples came to Jesus, saying unto him, "Where wilt thou that we prepare for thee to eat the passover?" And he sent Peter and John, saying, "Go ye into the city, and there shall meet you a man bearing a pitcher of water: follow him. And wheresoever he shall go in, say ye to the goodman of the house, The Master saith, Where is the guest-chamber, where I shall eat the passover with my disciples? And he will show you a large upper room, furnished and prepared: there make ready for us." And his disciples went forth, and came into the city, and found as he had said unto them: and they made ready the passover.

Jesus sends two disciples to make ready the passover

Now when the even was come, Jesus sat down with the twelve. And when he knew that his hour was come that he should depart out of this world unto the Father, having loved his own which The Last Supper. were in the world, he loved them unto the end. And he said unto them, " With desire I have desired to eat this passover with you before I suffer: for I say unto you, I will not any more eat thereof, until it be fulfilled in the kingdom of God."

And supper being ended, there was also a strife among them, which of them should be accounted the greatest. Jesus knowing that the Father had given all things into his hands, and that he was come from God, and went to God; he riseth from supper, and laid aside his garments; and took a towel, and girded himself. After that he poureth water into a Jesus washes the feet of the dis-ciples. basin, and began to wash the disciples' feet, and to wipe them with the towel wherewith he was girded. Then cometh he to Simon Peter: and Peter saith unto him, " Lord, dost thou wash my feet?" Jesus answered and said unto him, " What I do thou knowest not now; but thou shalt know hereafter." Peter saith unto him, " Thou shalt never wash my feet." Jesus answered him, " If I wash thee not, thou hast no part with me." Simon Peter saith unto him, " Lord, not my feet only, but also my hands and my head." Jesus saith to him, " He that is washed needeth not save to wash his feet, but is clean every whit: and ye are clean, but not all." For he knew who should betray him; therefore said he, " Ye are not all clean."

So after he had washed their feet, and had taken his garments, and was set down again, he said unto them, " Know ye what I have done to you? The kings of the Gentiles exercise lordship over them; and they that exercise authority upon them are called benefactors. But ye shall not be so: but he that is greatest among you, let him be as the younger: and he that is chief, as he that doth serve. For whether is greater, he that sitteth at meat, or he that serveth? is not he that sitteth at meat? but I am among you as he that serveth. Ye call me Master and Lord: and ye say well; for so I am. If I then, your Lord and Master, have washed your feet; ye also ought to wash one another's feet. For I have given you an example, that ye should do as I have done to you. Verily, verily, I say unto you, The servant is not greater than his lord; neither he that is sent greater than he that sent him. If ye know these things, happy are ye if ye do them. Ye are they which have continued with me in my temptations. And I appoint unto you a kingdom, as my Father hath appointed unto me; that ye may eat and drink at my table in my kingdom, and sit on thrones judging the twelve tribes of Israel. I speak not of you all: I know whom I have chosen: but that the scripture may be fulfilled, He that eateth bread with me hath lifted up his heel against me. Now I tell you before it

come, that, when it is come to pass, ye may believe that I am he. Verily, verily, I say unto you, He that receiveth whomsoever I send receiveth me; and he that receiveth me receiveth him that sent me."

When Jesus had thus said, (the devil having now put into the heart of Judas Iscariot, Simon's son, to betray him,) he was troubled in spirit, and testified, and said, "Verily, verily, I say unto you, that one of you shall betray me." Then the disciples looked one on another, doubt- <small>He predicts that Judas will betray him.</small> ing of whom he spake. And they were exceeding sorrowful, and began every one of them to say unto him, "Lord, is it I?" Now there was leaning on Jesus' bosom one of his disciples, whom Jesus loved. Simon Peter therefore beckoned to him, that he should ask who it should be of whom he spake. He then lying on Jesus' breast saith unto him, "Lord, who is it?" Jesus answered, "He it is, to whom I shall give a sop, when I have dipped it. The Son of man goeth as it is written of him: but woe unto that man by whom the Son of man is betrayed! it had been good for that man if he had not been born." And when he had dipped the sop, he gave it to Judas Iscariot, the son of Simon. And after the sop Satan entered into him. Then said Jesus unto him, "That thou doest, do quickly." Now no man at the table knew for what intent he spake this unto him. For some of them thought, because Judas had the bag, that Jesus had said unto him, Buy those things that we have need of against the feast; or, that he should give something to the poor. He then having received the sop went immediately out: and it was night. Therefore, when he was gone out, Jesus said, "Now is the Son of man glorified, and God is glorified in him. If God be glorified in him, God shall also glorify him in himself, and shall straightway glorify him. Little children, yet a little while I am with you. Ye shall seek me: and as I said unto the Jews, Whither I go, ye cannot come; so now I say to you. A new commandment I give unto you, That ye love one another; as I have loved you, that ye also love one another. By this shall all men know that ye are my disciples, if ye have love one to another."

And as they were eating, Jesus took bread, and when he had given thanks, he brake it, and gave it to the disciples, and said, "Take, eat; this is my body which is given for you: this do in remembrance <small>The Lord's supper instituted.</small> of me." After the same manner also he took the cup after supper, and gave thanks, and gave it to them, saying, "Drink ye all of it; for this is my blood of the new testament, which is shed for many for the remission of sins. This do as often as ye drink it in remembrance of me. Verily I say unto you, I will not drink henceforth of this fruit of the vine, until that day when I drink it new with you in my Father's kingdom." And they all drank of it.

Simon Peter said unto him, "Lord, whither goest thou?" Jesus answered him, " Whither I go, thou canst not follow me now; but thou shalt follow me afterwards." Peter said unto him, Lord, why cannot I follow thee now? I will lay down my life for thy sake." Then saith Jesus unto them, " All ye shall be offended because of me this night: for it is written, I will smite the shepherd, and the sheep of the flock shall be scattered abroad. But after I am risen again, I will go before you into Galilee." Peter answered and said unto him, "Though all men shall be offended because of thee, yet will I never be offended." And the Lord said, " Simon, Simon, behold, Satan hath desired to have you, that he may sift you as wheat: but I have prayed for thee, that thy faith fail not: and when thou art converted, strengthen thy brethren." And he said unto him, " Lord, I am ready to go with thee, both into prison, and to death." And he said,

He prophesieth that Peter will deny him. " I tell thee, Peter, That this day, even in this night, before the cock crow twice, thou shalt deny me thrice." But he spake the more vehemently, " If I should die with thee, I will not deny thee in any wise." Likewise also said they all.

And he said unto them, " When I sent you without purse, and scrip, and shoes, lacked ye anything?" And they said, " Nothing." Then said he unto them, " But now, he that hath a purse, let him take it, and likewise his scrip: and he that hath no sword, let him sell his garment, and buy

He again foretells his death. one. For I say unto you, that this that is written must yet be accomplished in me, And he was reckoned among the transgressors: for the things concerning me have an end." And they said, " Lord, behold, here are two swords." And he said unto them, " It is enough."

CHAPTER XXXVII.

THE LAST ADDRESS OF JESUS TO HIS DISCIPLES.

ET not your heart be troubled: ye believe in God, believe also in me. In my Father's house are many mansions: if it were not so, I would have told you. I go to prepare a place for you. And if I go and prepare a place for you, I will come again, and receive you unto myself; that where I am, there ye may be also. And whither I go ye know, and the way ye know."

Thomas saith unto him, "Lord, we know not whither thou goest; and how can we know the way?" Jesus saith unto him, "I am the way, the truth, and the life: no man cometh unto the Father, but by me. If ye had known me, ye should have known my Father also: and from henceforth ye know him, and have seen him."

He comforts his disciples.

Philip saith unto him, "Lord, show us the Father, and it sufficeth us." Jesus saith unto him, "Have I been so long time with you, and yet hast thou not known me, Philip? he that hath seen me hath seen the Father; and how sayest thou then, Show us the Father? believest thou not that I am in the Father, and the Father in me? the words that I speak unto you I speak not of myself: but the Father that dwelleth in me, he doeth the works. Believe me that I am in the Father, and the Father in me: or else believe me for the very works' sake. Verily, verily, I say unto you, He that believeth on me, the works that I do shall he do also; and greater works than these shall he do; because I go unto my Father. And whatsoever ye shall ask in my name, that will I do, that the Father may be glorified in the Son.

He declareth his oneness with the Father.

"If ye shall ask anything in my name, I will do it. If ye love me, keep my commandments. And I will pray the Father, and he shall give you another Comforter, that he may abide with you forever; even the Spirit of truth; whom the world cannot receive, because it seeth him not, neither knoweth him: but ye know him; for he dwelleth with you, and shall be in you. I will not leave you comfortless: I will come to you. Yet a little while, and the world seeth me no more; but ye see me: because I live,

THE WAY, THE TRUTH, THE LIFE.

ye shall live also. At that day ye shall know that I am in my Father, and ye in me, and I in you. He that hath my commandments, and keepeth them, he it is that loveth me: and he that loveth me shall be loved of my Father, and I will love him, and will manifest myself to him." Judas saith unto him, not Iscariot, "Lord, how is it that thou wilt manifest thyself unto us, and not unto the world?"

Jesus answered and saith unto him, "If a man love me, he will keep my words: and my Father will love him, and we will come unto him, and *He promises the Holy Ghost to them.* make our abode with him. He that loveth me not keepeth not my sayings: and the word which ye hear is not mine, but the Father's which sent me. These things have I spoken unto you, being yet present with you. But the Comforter, which is the Holy Ghost, whom the Father will send in my name, he shall teach you all things, and bring all things to your remembrance, whatsoever I have said unto you. Peace I leave with you, my peace I give unto you: not as the world giveth, give I unto you. Let not your heart be troubled, neither let it be afraid. Ye have heard how I said unto you, I go away, and come again unto you. If ye loved me, ye would rejoice, because I said, I go unto the Father: for my Father is greater than I. And now I have told you before it come to pass, that, when it is come to pass, ye might believe. Hereafter I will not talk much with you: for the prince of this world cometh, and hath nothing in me. But that the world may know that I love the Father; and as the Father gave me commandment, even so I do. Arise, let us go hence.

"I am the true vine, and my Father is the husbandman. Every branch *The parable of the vine and the branches.* in me that beareth not fruit he taketh away: and every branch that beareth fruit, he purgeth it, that it may bring forth more fruit. Now ye are clean through the word which I have spoken unto you. Abide in me, and I in you. As the branch cannot bear fruit of itself, except it abide in the vine; no more can ye, except ye abide in me. I am the vine, ye are the branches: He that abideth in me, and I in him, the same bringeth forth much fruit: for without me ye can do nothing. If a man abide not in me, he is cast forth as a branch, and is withered; and men gather them, and cast them into the fire, and they are burned. If ye abide in me, and my words abide in you, ye shall ask what ye will, and it shall be done unto you. Herein is my Father glorified, that ye bear much fruit; so shall ye be my disciples. As the Father hath loved me, so have I loved you: continue ye in my love. If ye keep my commandments, ye shall abide in my love; even as I have kept my Father's commandments, and abide in his love. These things have I spoken unto you, that my joy might remain in you, and that your joy might be full. This is my commandment, That ye love one another, as I have loved you. Greater love hath no man than this, that a man lay down his life for his friends. Ye are my friends, if ye do whatsoever I command you. Henceforth I call you not servants; for the servant knoweth not what his lord doeth: but I have called you friends; for all things that I have heard of my Father I have made known unto you. Ye have not chosen me, but I have chosen you, and ordained you, that ye should go and bring forth fruit, and that your fruit should remain: that whatsoever ye shall ask of the Father in my name, he may give it you. These things I command you, that ye love one another. If the world hate you, ye know that it hated me before it hated you. If ye were of the world, the world would love his own: but because ye are not of the world, but I have chosen *He prophesieth persecutions.* you out of the world, therefore the world hateth you. Remember the word that I said unto you, The servant is not greater than his lord. If they have persecuted me, they will also persecute you; if they have kept my saying, they will keep yours also. But all these things will they do unto you for my name's sake, because they know not him that sent me. If I had not come and spoken unto them, they had not had sin; but now they have no cloke for their sin. He that hateth me hateth my Father also. If I had not done among them the works which none other man did, they had not had sin: but now have they both seen and hated both me and my Father. But this cometh to pass, that the word might be fulfilled that is written in their law, They hated me without a cause. But *The Comforter promised.* when the Comforter is come, whom I will send unto you from the Father, even the Spirit of truth, which proceedeth from the Father, he shall testify of me: and ye also shall bear witness, because ye have been with me from the beginning.

"These things have I spoken unto you, that ye should not be offended. They shall put you out of the synagogues: yea, the time cometh, that whosoever killeth you will think that he doeth God service. And these things will they do unto you, because they have not known the Father, nor me. But these things have I told you, that when the time shall come, ye may remember that I told you of them. And these things I said not unto you at the beginning, because I was with you. But now I go my way to him that sent me; and none of you asketh me, Whither goest thou? but because I have said these things unto you, sorrow hath filled your heart. Nevertheless I tell you the truth. It is expedient for you that I go away: for if I go not away, the Comforter will not come unto you; but if I depart, I will send him unto you. And when he is come, he will reprove the world of sin, and of righteousness, and of judgment: of sin, because they believe not on me; of righteousness, because I go to my Father, and ye see me no more; of judgment, because the prince of this world is judged. I have yet many things to say unto you, but ye cannot bear them now. Howbeit when he, the Spirit of truth, is come, he will guide you into all truth: for

cc

he shall not speak of himself; but whatsoever he shall hear, that shall he speak: and he will show you things to come. He shall glorify me: for he shall receive of mine, and shall show it unto you. All things that the Father hath are mine: therefore said I, that he shall take of mine, and shall show it unto you. A little while, and ye shall not see me; and again, a little while, and ye shall see me, because I go to the Father."

Then said some of his disciples among themselves, "What is this that he saith unto us, A little while, and ye shall not see me: and again, a little while, and ye shall see me: and, Because I go to the Father?" They said therefore, "What is this that he saith, A little while? we cannot tell what he saith."

Now Jesus knew that they were desirous to ask him, and said unto them, "Do ye inquire among yourselves of that I said, A little while, and ye shall not see me: and again, a little while, and ye shall see me? Verily, verily, I say unto you, That ye shall weep and lament, but the world shall rejoice: and ye shall be sorrowful, but your sorrow shall be turned into joy. A woman when she is in travail *He predicts his resurrection* hath sorrow, because her hour is come: but as soon as she is delivered of the child, she remembereth no more the anguish, for joy that a man is born into the world. And ye now therefore have sorrow: but I will see you again, and your heart shall rejoice, and your joy no man taketh from you. And in that day ye shall ask me nothing. Verily, verily, I say unto you, Whatsoever ye shall ask the Father in my name, he will give it you. Hitherto have ye asked nothing in my name: ask, and ye shall receive, that your joy may be full. These things have I spoken unto you in proverbs: but the time cometh, when I shall no more speak unto you in proverbs, but I shall show you plainly of the Father. At that day ye shall ask in my name: and I say not unto you, that I will pray the Father for you: for the Father himself loveth you, because ye have loved me, and have believed that I came out from God. I came forth from the Father, and am come into the world: again, I leave the world, and go to the Father." His disciples said unto him, "Lo, now speakest thou plainly, and speakest no proverb. Now are we sure that thou knowest all things, and needest not that any man should ask thee: by this we believe that thou camest forth from God." Jesus answered them, "Do ye *Last words* now believe? behold, the hour cometh, yea, is now come, that ye shall be scattered, every man to his own, and shall leave me alone: and yet I am not alone, because the Father is with me. These things I have spoken unto you, that in me ye might have peace. In the world ye shall have tribulation: but be of good cheer; I have overcome the world."

CHAPTER XXXVIII.

THE LAST PRAYER OF CHRIST.

THESE words spake Jesus, and lifted up his eyes to heaven, and said, "Father, the hour is come; glorify thy Son, that thy Son also may glorify thee: as thou hast given him power over all flesh, that he should give eternal life to as many as thou hast given him. And this is life eternal, that they might know thee the only true God, and Jesus Christ, whom thou hast sent. I have glorified thee on the earth: I have finished the work which thou gavest me to do. And now, O Father, glorify thou me with thine own self with the glory which I had with thee before the world was. I have manifested thy name unto the men which thou gavest me out of the world: thine they were, and thou gavest them me; and they have kept thy word. Now they have known that all things whatsoever thou hast given me are of thee. For I have given unto them the words which thou gavest me; and they have received them, and have known surely that I came out from thee, and they have believed that thou didst send me. I pray for them: I pray not for the world, but for them which thou hast given me; for they are thine. And all mine are thine, and thine are mine; and I am glorified in them. And now I am no more in the world, but these are in the world, and I come to thee. Holy Father, keep through thine own name those whom thou hast given me, that they may be one, as we are. While I was with them in the world, I kept them in thy name: those that thou gavest me I have kept, and none of them is lost, but the son of perdition; that the scripture might be fulfilled. And now come I to thee; and these things I speak in the world, that they might have my joy fulfilled in themselves. I have given them thy word; and the world hath hated them, because they are not of the world, even as I am not of the world. I pray not that thou shouldest take them out of the world, but that thou shouldest keep them from the evil. They are not of the world, even as I am not of the world. Sanctify them through thy truth: thy word is truth. As thou hast sent me into the world, even so have I also sent them into the world. And for their sakes I

THE SLEEP OF THE DISCIPLES.

233

sanctify myself, that they also might be sanctified through the truth. Neither pray I for these alone, but for them also which shall believe on me through their word; that they all may be one; as thou, Father, art in me, and I in thee, that they also may be one in us: that the world may believe that thou hast sent me. And the glory which thou gavest me I have given them; that they may be one, even as we are one: I in them, and thou in me, that they may be made perfect in one; and that the world may know that thou hast sent me, and hast loved them, as thou hast loved me. Father, I will that they also, whom thou hast given me, be with me where I am; that they may behold my glory, which thou hast given me: for thou lovedst me before the foundation of the world. O righteous Father, the world hath not known thee: but I have known thee, and these have known that thou hast sent me. And I have declared unto them thy name, and will declare it: that the love wherewith thou hast loved me may be in them, and I in them."

And when they had sung an hymn, they went out over the brook Cedron, into the mount of Olives. Then cometh Jesus with them unto a place called Gethsemane, where was a garden, into the which he entered, and his disciples. And he saith unto the disciples, "Sit ye here, while I go and pray yonder." And he took with him Peter and the two sons of Zebedee, and began to be sorrowful and very heavy. Then saith he unto them, "My soul is exceeding sorrowful, even unto death: tarry ye here, and watch with me." And he went a little farther, and fell on his face, and prayed, saying, "O my Father, if it be possible, let this cup pass from me: nevertheless not as I will, but as thou wilt." And when he rose up from prayer, and was come to his disciples, he found them sleeping for sorrow. And he saith unto Peter, "What, could ye not watch with me one hour? watch and pray, that ye enter not into temptation: the spirit indeed is willing, but the flesh is weak." He went away again the second time, and prayed, saying, "O my Father, if this cup may not pass away from me, except I drink it, thy will be done." And he came and found them asleep again, (for their eyes were heavy,) neither wist they what to answer him. And he left them, and went away again, and prayed the third time, saying the same words. And there appeared an angel unto him from heaven, strengthening him. And being in an agony he prayed more earnestly: and his sweat was as it were great drops of blood falling down to the ground. Then cometh he to his disciples, and saith unto them, "Sleep on now, and take your rest: behold, the hour is at hand, and the Son of man is betrayed into the hands of sinners. Rise, let us be going: behold, he is at hand that doth betray me."

And while he yet spake, lo, Judas, (which betrayed him, for he knew the place: for Jesus ofttimes resorted thither with his disciples,) one of the

The agony in the garden of Gethsemane.

JUDAS GUIDES THE SOLDIERS.

twelve, came, and with him a great multitude with lanterns and torches and swords and staves, from the chief priests and elders of the people. Jesus therefore, knowing all things that should come upon him,

The betrayal and arrest. went forth, and said unto them, "Whom seek ye?" They answered him, "Jesus of Nazareth." Jesus saith unto them, "I am he." And Judas also, which betrayed him, stood with them. As soon then as he had said unto them, "I am he," they went backward, and fell to the ground. Then asked he them again, "Whom seek ye?" And they said, "Jesus of Nazareth." Jesus answered, "I have told you that I am he: if therefore ye seek me, let these go their way"; that the saying might be fulfilled, which he spake, "Of them which thou gavest me have I lost none." Now he that betrayed him gave them a sign, saying, "Whomsoever I shall kiss, that same is he: hold him fast." And forthwith he came to Jesus, and said, "Hail, Master"; and kissed him. And Jesus said unto him, "Friend, wherefore art thou come? Judas, betrayest thou the Son of man with a kiss?" Then the band and the captain and officers of the Jews took Jesus, and bound him. When they which were about him saw

Peter smites with the sword. what would follow, they said unto him, "Lord, shall we smite with the sword?" Then Simon Peter having a sword drew it, and smote the high-priest's servant, and cut off his right ear. The servant's name was Malchus. Then said Jesus unto Peter, "Put up thy sword into the sheath: the cup which my Father hath given me, shall I not drink it? for all they that take the sword shall perish with the sword. Thinkest thou that I cannot now pray to my Father, and he shall presently give me more than twelve legions of angels? but how then shall the scriptures be fulfilled, that thus it must be? Suffer ye thus far." And he touched Malchus' ear, and healed him.

Then Jesus said unto the chief priests, and captains of the temple, and the elders, which were come to him, "Be ye come out, as against a thief,

Jesus is deserted. with swords and staves? when I was daily with you in the temple, ye stretched forth no hands against me: but this is your hour, and the power of darkness." Then all the disciples forsook him, and fled.

And there followed him a certain young man, having a linen cloth cast about his naked body; and the young men laid hold on him: and he left the linen cloth, and fled from them naked.

CHAPTER XXXIX.

JESUS IS TRIED AND CONDEMNED.

ND they that had laid hold on Jesus led him away to Annas first: for he was father-in-law to Caiaphas, which was the high-priest that same year. Now Caiaphas was he, which gave counsel to the Jews, that it was expedient that one man should die for the people. Now Annas had sent him bound unto Caiaphas the high-priest. And Simon Peter followed Jesus afar off, and so did another disciple: that disciple was known unto the high-priest, and went in with Jesus into the palace of the high-priest. But Peter stood at the door without. Then went out that other disciple, which was known unto the high-priest, and spake unto her that kept the door, and brought in Peter. And the servants and officers stood there, who had made a fire of coals; for it was cold: and they warmed themselves: and Peter went in and warmed himself, and sat with the servants, to see the end.

He is taken before the high-priest.

And as Peter was beneath in the palace, there cometh the damsel that kept the door. And when she saw Peter warming himself, she earnestly looked upon him, and said, "Art not thou also one of this man's disciples?" But he denied, saying, "I know not, neither understand I what thou sayest." And he went out into the porch; and the cock crew.

Peter denieth him.

And a maid saw him again, and began to say to them that stood by, "This is one of them." And he denied it again. And about the space of one hour after, they that stood by said again to Peter, "Surely thou art one of them: for thou art a Galilean, and thy speech agreeth thereto." But he began to curse and to swear, saying, "I know not this man of whom ye speak."

And immediately, while he yet spake, the second time the cock crew. And the Lord turned, and looked upon Peter. And Peter called to mind the word that Jesus said unto him, "Before the cock crow twice, thou shalt deny me thrice." And when he thought thereon, he went out, and wept bitterly.

THE DENIAL OF PETER

The high-priest then asked Jesus of his disciples, and of his doctrine. Jesus answered him, "I spake openly to the world; I ever taught in the synagogue, and in the temple, whither the Jews always resort; and in secret have I said nothing. Why askest thou me? ask them which heard me, what I have said unto them: behold, they know what I said." And when he had thus spoken, one of the officers which stood by struck Jesus with the palm of his hand, saying, "Answerest thou the high-priest so?" Jesus answered him, "If I have spoken evil, bear witness of the evil: but if well, why smitest thou me?"

Jesus is examined by the high-priest.

And as soon as it was day, the elders of the people and the chief priests and the scribes came together, and led him into their council. And the chief priests and all the council sought for witness against Jesus to put him to death: and found none. For many bare false witness against him, but their witness agreed not together. And there arose certain, and bare false witness against him, saying, "We heard him say, I will destroy this temple that is made with hands, and within three days I will build another made without hands." But neither so did their witness agree together. And the high-priest stood up in the midst, and asked Jesus, saying, "Answerest thou nothing? what is it which these witness against thee?" But he held his peace, and answered nothing. Again the high-priest asked him, and said unto him, "I adjure thee by the living God, that thou tell us whether thou be the Christ, the Son of God." Jesus saith unto him, "I am: and ye shall see the Son of man sitting on the right hand of power, and coming in the clouds of heaven." Then said they all, "Art thou then the Son of God?" And he said unto them, "Ye say that I am." Then the high-priest rent his clothes, saying, "He hath spoken blasphemy; what further need have we of witnesses? behold, now ye have heard his blasphemy. What think ye?" They answered and said, "He is guilty of death."

He is examined before the Sanhedrim.

And the men that held Jesus mocked him, and smote him. And some began to spit on him, and to cover his face, and to buffet him, and to say unto him, "Prophesy unto us, thou Christ, who is he that smote thee?" And many other things blasphemously spake they against him.

Jesus is mocked and buffeted.

When the morning was come, all the chief priests and elders of the people took counsel against Jesus to put him to death: and when they had bound him, they led him away from Caiaphas unto the hall of judgment: and delivered him to Pontius Pilate the governor. And they themselves went not into the judgment hall, lest they should be defiled; but that they might eat the passover. Pilate then went out unto them, and said, "What accusation bring ye against this man?" They answered and said unto him, "If he were not a malefactor, we would

He is accused before the Roman governor.

THE REPENTANCE OF PETER   27

not have delivered him up unto thee." Then said Pilate unto them, "Take ye him, and judge him according to your law." The Jews therefore said unto him, "It is not lawful for us to put any man to death": that the saying of Jesus might be fulfilled, which he spake, signifying what death he should die. And they began to accuse him, saying, "We found this fellow perverting the nation, and forbidding to give tribute to Cæsar, saying that he himself is Christ a king." Then Pilate entered into the judgment hall again, and called Jesus, and said unto him, "Art thou the King of the Jews?" Jesus answered him, "Sayest thou this thing of thyself, or did others tell it thee of me?" Pilate answered, "Am I a Jew? Thine own nation and the chief priests have delivered thee unto me: what hast thou done?" Jesus answered, "My kingdom is not of this world: if my kingdom were of this world, then would my servants fight, that I should not be delivered to the Jews: but now is my kingdom not from hence." Pilate therefore said unto him, "Art thou a king then?" Jesus answered, "Thou sayest that I am a king. To this end was I born, and for this cause came I into the world, that I should bear witness unto the truth. Every one that is of the truth heareth my voice." Pilate saith unto him, "What is truth?" And when he had said this, he went out again unto the Jews, and saith unto them, "I find in him no fault at all." And they were the more fierce, saying, "He stirreth up the people, teaching throughout all Jewry, beginning from Galilee to this place."

When Pilate heard of Galilee, he asked whether the man were a Galilean. And as soon as he knew that he belonged unto Herod's jurisdiction, he sent him to Herod, who himself also was at Jerusalem at that time. And when Herod saw Jesus, he was exceeding glad: for he was desirous to see him of a long season, because he had heard many things of him; and he hoped to have seen some miracle done by him. Then he questioned with him in many words; but he answered him nothing. And the chief priests and scribes stood and vehemently accused him. And Herod with his men of war set him at naught, and mocked him, and arrayed him in a gorgeous robe, and sent him again to Pilate. And the same day Pilate and Herod were made friends together: for before they were at enmity between themselves.

And Pilate, when he had called together the chief priests and the rulers and the people, said unto them, "Ye have brought this man unto me, as one that perverteth the people: and, behold, I, having examined him before you, have found no fault in this man touching those things whereof ye accuse him: no, nor yet Herod: for I sent you to him; and, lo, nothing worthy of death is done unto him. I will therefore chastise him, and release him."

Now at that feast the governor was wont to release unto the people a

[margin note] Pilate sends him to Herod.

[margin note] Pilate seeks to release Jesus.

JESUS BROUGHT BEFORE PILATE.

prisoner, whom they would. And there was one named Barabbas, which lay bound with them that had made insurrection with him, who had committed murder in the insurrection. And the multitude crying aloud began to desire him to do as he had ever done unto them. But Pilate answered them, saying, "Whom will ye that I release unto you? Barabbas, or Jesus which is called Christ?" For he knew that for envy they had delivered him. When he was set down on the judgment seat, his wife sent unto him, saying, "Have thou nothing to do with that just man: for I have suffered many things this day in a dream because of him." But the chief priests and elders persuaded the multitude that they should ask Barabbas, and destroy Jesus. The governor answered and said unto them, "Whether of the twain will ye that I release unto you?" They said, "Barabbas." Pilate saith unto them, "What shall I do then with Jesus which is called Christ?" But they cried, saying, "Crucify him, crucify him." And he said unto them the third time, "Why, what evil hath he done? I have found no cause of death in him: I will therefore chastise him, and let him go." And they cried out the more exceedingly, "Crucify him." And the voices of them and of the chief priests prevailed.

The multitude demand that he shall be crucified.

Then Pilate therefore took Jesus, and scourged him. And the soldiers of the governor took Jesus into the common hall, and gathered unto him the whole band of soldiers. And they stripped him, and put on him a scarlet robe. And when they had platted a crown of thorns, they put it upon his head, and a reed in his right hand: and they bowed the knee before him, and mocked him, saying, "Hail, king of the Jews!" And they spit upon him, and took the reed, and smote him on the head.

Jesus is scourged and mocked.

Pilate therefore went forth again, and saith unto them, "Behold, I bring him forth to you, that ye may know that I find no fault in him." Then came Jesus forth, wearing the crown of thorns, and the purple robe. And Pilate saith unto them, "Behold the man!" When the chief priests therefore and officers saw him, they cried out, saying, "Crucify him, crucify him." Pilate saith unto them, "Take ye him, and crucify him: for I find no fault in him." The Jews answered him, "We have a law, and by our law he ought to die, because he made himself the Son of God."

Pilate again seeks to release him.

When Pilate therefore heard that saying, he was the more afraid; and went again into the judgment hall, and saith unto Jesus, "Whence art thou?" But Jesus gave him no answer. Then saith Pilate unto him, "Speakest thou not unto me? knowest thou not that I have power to crucify thee, and have power to release thee?" Jesus answered, "Thou couldest have no power at all against me, except it were given thee from above: therefore he that delivered me unto thee hath the greater sin." And from thenceforth Pilate sought to release him: but the Jews cried out,

JESUS DELIVERED TO THE SOLDIERS.

saying, "If thou let this man go, thou art not Cæsar's friend: whosoever maketh himself a king speaketh against Cæsar."

When Pilate therefore heard that saying, he brought Jesus forth, and sat down in the judgment seat in a place that is called the Pavement, but in the Hebrew, Gabbatha. And it was the preparation of the passover, and about the sixth hour: and he saith unto the Jews, "Behold your King!" But they cried out, "Away with him, away with him, crucify him." Pilate saith unto them, "Shall I crucify your King?" The chief priests answered, "We have no king but Cæsar."

When Pilate saw that he could prevail nothing, but that rather a tumult was made, he took water, and washed his hands before the multitude, saying, "I am innocent of the blood of this just person: see ye to it." Then answered all the people, and said, "His blood be on us, and on our children." And he released unto them him that for sedition and murder was cast into prison, whom they had desired; but he delivered Jesus to their will. And after that they had mocked him, they took the robe off from him, and put his own raiment on him, and led him away to crucify him.

Jesus is delivered to be crucified.

Then Judas, which had betrayed him, when he saw that he was condemned, repented himself, and brought again the thirty pieces of silver to the chief priests and elders, saying, "I have sinned in that I have betrayed the innocent blood." And they said, "What is that to us? see thou to that." And he cast down the pieces of silver in the temple, and departed, and went and hanged himself. And the chief priests took the silver pieces, and said, "It is not lawful for to put them into the treasury, because it is the price of blood." And they took counsel, and bought with them the potter's field, to bury strangers in. Wherefore that field was called, "The field of blood," unto this day. Then was fulfilled that which was spoken by Jeremiah the prophet, saying, "And they took the thirty pieces of silver, the price of him that was valued, whom they of the children of Israel did value; and gave them for the potter's field, as the Lord appointed me."

Judas commits suicide.

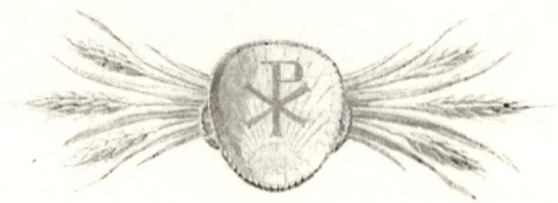

GOING FORTH TO CALVARY.

CHAPTER XL.

ND Jesus, bearing his cross, went forth. And as they led him away, they laid hold upon one Simon a Cyrenian, who passed by, coming out of the country, the father of Alexander and Rufus, and on him they laid the cross, that he might bear it after Jesus. And there followed him a great company of people, and of women, which also bewailed and lamented him. But Jesus turning unto them said, "Daughters of Jerusalem, weep not for me, but weep for yourselves, and for your children. For, behold, the days are coming, in the which they shall say, Blessed are the barren, and the wombs that never bare, and the paps which never gave suck. Then shall they begin to say to the mountains, Fall on us; and to the hills, Cover us. For if they do these things in a green tree, what shall be done in the dry?" And there were also two other, malefactors, led with him to be put to death. And when they were come unto a place called Golgotha, that is to say, a place of a skull, they gave him vinegar to drink mingled with gall: and when he had tasted thereof, he would not drink.

Jesus is led away to Golgotha

And the soldiers crucified him, and took his garments, and made four parts, to every soldier a part; and also his coat: now the coat was without seam, woven from the top throughout. They said therefore among themselves, "Let us not rend it, but cast lots for it, whose it shall be": that the scripture might be fulfilled, which saith, "They parted my raiment among them, and for my vesture they did cast lots." These things therefore the soldiers did. And Pilate wrote a title, and put it on the cross. And the writing was,

He is crucified.

JESUS OF NAZARETH THE KING OF THE JEWS.

This title then read many of the Jews: for the place where Jesus was crucified was nigh to the city: and it was written in Hebrew, and Greek, and Latin. Then said the chief priests of the Jews to Pilate, "Write not, The King of the Jews; but that he said, I am King of the

THE CRUCIFIXION. 245

Jews." Pilate answered, "What I have written I have written." And it was the third hour, and they crucified him. And with him they crucify two thieves; the one on his right hand, and the other on his left. And the scripture was fulfilled, which saith, "And he was numbered with the transgressors." Then said Jesus, "Father, forgive them; for they know not what they do." And they parted his raiment, and cast lots. And the people stood beholding. And they that passed by reviled him, wagging their heads, and saying, "Thou that destroyest the temple, and buildest it in three days, save thyself. If thou be the Son of God, come down from the cross." Likewise also the chief priests mocking him, with the scribes and elders, said, "He saved others; himself he cannot save. If he be the King of Israel, let him now come down from the cross, and we will believe him. He trusted in God; let him deliver him now, if he will have him: for he said, I am the Son of God." And the soldiers also mocked him, coming to him, and offering him vinegar, and saying, "If thou be the king of the Jews, save thyself."

And one of the malefactors which were hanged railed on him, saying, "If thou be Christ, save thyself and us." But the other answering rebuked him, saying, "Dost not thou fear God, seeing thou art in the same condemnation? and we indeed justly; for we receive the due reward of our deeds: but this man hath done nothing amiss." And he said unto Jesus, "Lord, remember me when thou comest into thy kingdom." And Jesus said unto him, "Verily I say unto thee, To-day shalt thou be with me in paradise."

Now there stood by the cross of Jesus his mother, and his mother's sister, Mary the wife of Cleophas, and Mary Magdalene. When Jesus therefore saw his mother, and the disciple standing by, whom he loved, he saith unto his mother, "Woman, behold thy son!" Then saith he to the disciple, "Behold thy mother!" And from that hour that disciple took her unto his own home.

Now from the sixth hour there was darkness over all the land unto the ninth hour. And about the ninth hour Jesus cried with a loud voice, saying, "Eli, Eli, lama sabachthani?" that is to say, "My God, my God, why hast thou forsaken me?" Some of them that stood there, when they heard that, said, "This man calleth for Elijah." After this, Jesus, knowing that all things were now accomplished, that the scripture might be fulfilled, saith, "I thirst." Now there was set a vessel full of vinegar: and straightway one of them ran, and took a sponge, and filled it with vinegar, and put it on a reed, and gave him to drink. The rest said, "Let be, let us see whether Elijah will come to save him." Jesus, when he had cried again with a loud voice, said, "It is finished;

AFTER THE CRUCIFIXION.

Father, into thy hands I commend my spirit": and having said thus, he bowed his head, and gave up the ghost.

And, behold, the veil of the temple was rent in twain from the top to the bottom; and the earth did quake, and the rocks rent; and the graves were opened; and many bodies of the saints which slept arose, and came out of the graves after his resurrection, and went into the holy city, and appeared unto many. Now when the centurion, and they that were with him, watching Jesus, saw the earthquake, and that he so cried out, and gave up the ghost, they feared greatly, saying, "Truly this was the Son of God." And all the people that came together to that sight, beholding the things which were done, smote their breasts, and returned.

The signs which followed.

And all his acquaintance, and the women, stood afar off, beholding these things, among which was Mary Magdalene, and Mary the mother of James and Joses, and the mother of Zebedee's children, which followed Jesus from Galilee, ministering unto him: and many other women which came up with him unto Jerusalem.

The Jews therefore, because it was the preparation, that the bodies should not remain upon the cross on the sabbath day, (for that sabbath day was an high day,) besought Pilate that their legs might be broken, and that they might be taken away. Then came the soldiers, and brake the legs of the first, and of the other which was crucified with him. But when they came to Jesus, and saw that he was dead already, they brake not his legs: but one of the soldiers with a spear pierced his side, and forthwith came thereout blood and water. And he that saw it bare record, and his record is true: and he knoweth that he saith true, that ye might believe. For these things were done, that the scripture should be fulfilled, "A bone of him shall not be broken." And again another scripture saith, "They shall look on him whom they pierced."

The descent from the cross.

And now when the even was come, there came a rich man named Joseph, of Arimathea, a city of the Jews: a counselor; and he was a good man, and a just: who also himself waited for the kingdom of God: (the same had not consented to the counsel and deed of them.) Joseph being a disciple of Jesus, but secretly for fear of the Jews, came, and went in boldly unto Pilate, and craved the body of Jesus. And Pilate marveled if he were already dead: and calling unto him the centurion, he asked him whether he had been any while dead. And when he knew it of the centurion, he gave the body to Joseph. He came therefore, and took the body of Jesus. And there came also Nicodemus, which at the first came to Jesus by night, and brought a mixture of myrrh and aloes, about an hundred pound weight. Then took they the body of Jesus, and wound it in linen clothes with the spices, as the manner of the Jews is to bury.

The burial.

JOSEPH OF ARIMATHEA PREPARES CHRIST FOR BURIAL.

Now in the place where he was crucified there was a garden; and in the garden a new sepulcher, hewn out of a rock, wherein was never man yet laid. There laid they Jesus therefore because of the Jews' preparation day. And Joseph rolled a great stone to the door of the sepulcher, and departed. And the women also, which came with him from Galilee, followed after, and beheld the sepulcher, and how his body was laid. And they returned, and prepared spices and ointments; and rested the sabbath day according to the commandment. And there was Mary Magdalene, and the other Mary, sitting over against the sepulcher.

Now the next day, that followed the day of the preparation, the chief priests and Pharisees came together unto Pilate, saying, "Sir, we remember that that deceiver said, while he was yet alive, After three days I will rise again. Command therefore that the sepulcher be made sure until the third day, lest his disciples come by night, and steal him away, and say unto the people, He is risen from the dead: so the last A guard placed over the sepulcher. error shall be worse than the first." Pilate said unto them, "Ye have a watch: go your way, make it as sure as ye can." So they went, and made the sepulcher sure, sealing the stone, and setting a watch.

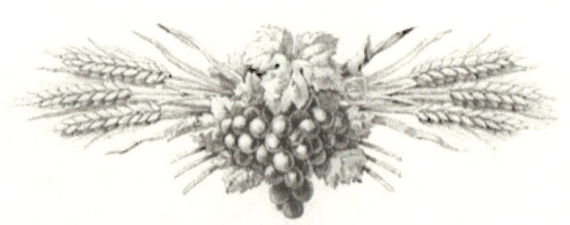

THE BURIAL OF CHRIST.

255

CHAPTER XLI

THE RESURRECTION.

AND when the sabbath was past, Mary Magdalene, and Mary the mother of James, and Salome, had bought sweet spices, that they might come and anoint him. And very early in the morning the first day of the week, they came unto the sepulcher at the rising of the sun. And, behold, there was a great earthquake: for the angel of the Lord descended from heaven, and came and rolled back the stone from the door, and sat upon it. His countenance was like lightning, and his raiment white as snow: and for fear of him the keepers did shake, and became as dead men.

The angel at the tomb.

And they said among themselves, "Who shall roll us away the stone from the door of the sepulcher?" And when they looked, they saw that the stone was rolled away: for it was very great. And entering into the sepulcher, they saw a young man sitting on the right side, clothed in a long white garment; and they were affrighted. And he saith unto them, "Be not affrighted. Ye seek Jesus of Nazareth, which was crucified: he is risen; he is not here: behold the place where they laid him. But go your way, tell his disciples and Peter that he goeth before you into Galilee: there shall ye see him, as he said unto you." And they departed quickly from the sepulcher with fear and great joy; and did run to bring his disciples word.

Then [Mary Magdalene] cometh to Simon Peter, and to the other disciple, whom Jesus loved, and saith unto them, "They have taken away the Lord out of the sepulcher, and we know not where they have laid him."

Peter therefore went forth, and that other disciple, and came to the sepulcher. So they ran both together: and the other disciple did outrun Peter, and came first to the sepulcher. And he stooping down, and looking in, saw the linen clothes lying; yet went he not in. Then cometh Simon Peter following him, and went into the sepulcher, and seeth the linen clothes lie, and the napkin, that was about his head, not

An empty tomb.

lying with the linen clothes, but wrapped together in a place by itself. Then went in also that other disciple, which came first to the sepulcher, and he saw, and believed. For as yet they knew not the scripture, that he must rise again from the dead.

Then the disciples went away again unto their own home. But Mary stood without at the sepulcher weeping: and as she wept, she stooped down, and looked into the sepulcher, and seeth two angels in white sitting, the one at the head, and the other at the feet, where the body of Jesus had lain. And they say unto her, "Woman, why weepest thou?" She saith unto them, "Because they have taken away my Lord, and I know not where they have laid him." And when she had thus said, she turned herself back, and saw Jesus standing, and knew not that it was Jesus. Jesus saith unto her, "Woman, why weepest thou? whom seekest thou?" She, supposing him to be the gardener, saith unto him, "Sir, if thou have borne him hence, tell me where thou hast laid him, and I will take him away." Jesus saith unto her, "Mary." She turned herself, and saith unto him, "Rabboni"; (which is to say, "Master.") Jesus saith unto her, "Touch me not; for I am not yet ascended to my Father: but go to my brethren, and say unto them, I ascend unto my Father, and your Father; and to my God, and your God."

Jesus appears to Mary Magdalene.

It was Mary Magdalene, and Joanna, and Mary the mother of James, and other women that were with them, which told these things unto the apostles. And as they went to tell his disciples, behold, Jesus met them, saying, "All hail." And they came and held him by the feet, and worshiped him. Then said Jesus unto them, "Be not afraid: go tell my brethren that they go into Galilee, and there shall they see me." And their words seemed to them as idle tales, and they believed them not.

The apostles do not believe.

Now some of the watch came into the city, and showed unto the chief priests all the things that were done. And when they were assembled with the elders, and had taken counsel, they gave large money unto the soldiers, saying, "Say ye, His disciples came by night, and stole him away while we slept. And if this come to the governor's ears, we will persuade him, and secure you." So they took the money, and did as they were taught: and this saying is commonly reported among the Jews until this day.

The story of the guard.

And, behold, two of the disciples went that same day to a village called Emmaus, which was from Jerusalem about threescore furlongs. And they talked together of all these things which had happened. And it came to pass, that, while they communed together and reasoned, Jesus himself drew near, and went with them. But their eyes were holden that they should not know him. And he said unto them, "What manner of communications

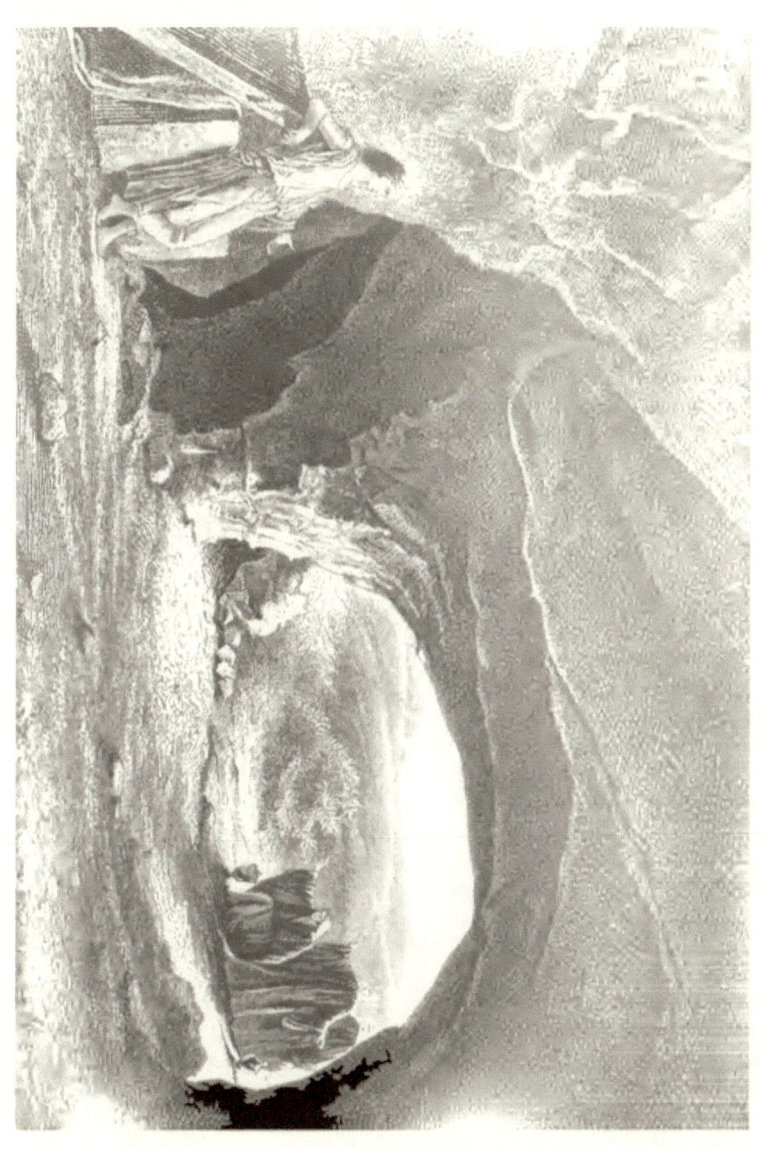

are these that ye have one to another, as ye walk, and are sad?" And the
one of them, whose name was Cleopas, answering said unto
him, "Art thou only a stranger in Jerusalem, and hast not
known the things which are come to pass there in these days?" And he
said unto them, "What things?" And they said unto him, "Concerning
Jesus of Nazareth, which was a prophet mighty in deed and word before
God and all the people: and how the chief priests and our rulers delivered
him to be condemned to death, and have crucified him. But we trusted
that it had been he which should have redeemed Israel: and beside all this,
to-day is the third day since these things were done. Yea, and certain
women also of our company made us astonished, which were early at the
sepulcher; and when they found not his body, they came, saying that they
had also seen a vision of angels, which said that he was alive. And certain of them which were with us went to the sepulcher, and found it even
so as the women had said: but him they saw not." Then he said unto
them, "O fools, and slow of heart to believe all that the prophets have
spoken: ought not Christ to have suffered these things, and to enter into
his glory?" And beginning at Moses and all the prophets, he expounded
unto them in all the scriptures the things concerning himself.

And they drew nigh unto the village, whither they went: and he made
as though he would have gone further. But they constrained him, saying,
"Abide with us: for it is toward evening, and the day is far spent." And
he went in to tarry with them. And it came to pass, as he sat at meat with
them, he took bread, and blessed it, and brake, and gave to them. And
their eyes were opened, and they knew him; and he vanished out of their
sight. And they said one to another, "Did not our heart burn within us,
while he talked with us by the way, and while he opened to us the scriptures?" And they rose up the same hour, and returned to Jerusalem, and
found the eleven gathered together, and them that were with them, saying,
"The Lord is risen indeed, and hath appeared to Simon." And they told
what things were done in the way, and how he was known of them in
breaking of bread.

And as they thus spake, Jesus himself stood in the midst of them,
and saith unto them, "Peace be unto you." But they were terrified and
affrighted, and supposed that they had seen a spirit. And he
said unto them, "Why are ye troubled? and why do thoughts
arise in your hearts? behold my hands and my feet, that it is I myself:
handle me, and see; for a spirit hath not flesh and bones, as ye see me
have." And when he had thus spoken, he showed them his hands and his
feet. And while they yet believed not for joy, and wondered, he said
unto them, "Have ye here any meat?" And they gave him a piece of a
broiled fish, and of an honeycomb. And he took it, and did eat before

THE DISCIPLES AT EMMAUS

them. Then said Jesus to them again, "Peace be unto you: as my Father hath sent me, even so send I you." And when he had said this, he breathed on them, and saith unto them, "Receive ye the Holy Ghost: whosesoever sins ye remit, they are remitted unto them; and whosesoever sins ye retain, they are retained."

But Thomas, one of the twelve, called Didymus, was not with them when Jesus came. The other disciples therefore said unto him, "We have seen the Lord." But he said unto them, "Except I shall see in his hands the print of the nails, and put my finger into the print of the nails, and thrust my hand into his side, I will not believe." And after eight days again his disciples were within, and Thomas with them: then came Jesus, the doors being shut, and stood in the midst, and said, "Peace be unto you." Then saith he to Thomas, "Reach hither thy finger, and behold my hands; and reach hither thy hand, and thrust it into my side: and He appeareth again and convinceth Thomas. be not faithless, but believing." And Thomas answered and said unto him, "My Lord and my God." Jesus saith unto him, "Thomas, because thou hast seen me, thou hast believed: blessed are they that have not seen, and yet have believed." And he upbraided them with their unbelief and hardness of heart, because they believed not them which had seen him after he was risen.

And he said unto them, "These are the words which I spake unto you, while I was yet with you, that all things must be fulfilled, which were written in the law of Moses, and in the prophets, and in the psalms, concerning me." Then opened he their understanding, that they might understand the scriptures, and said unto them, "Thus it is written, and thus it behoved Christ to suffer, and to rise from the dead the third day: and that repentance and remission of sins should be preached in his name among all nations, beginning at Jerusalem. And ye are witnesses of these things. He sends them to preach. Go ye therefore, and teach all nations, baptizing them in the name of the Father, and of the Son, and of the Holy Ghost: teaching them to observe all things whatsoever I have commanded you. He that believeth and is baptized shall be saved; but he that believeth not shall be damned. And, behold, I send the promise of my Father upon you: and these signs shall follow them that believe: In my name shall they cast out devils; they shall speak with new tongues; they shall take up serpents; and if they drink any deadly thing, it shall not hurt them; they shall lay hands on the sick, and they shall recover. But tarry ye in the city of Jerusalem, until ye be endued with power from on high. And, lo, I am with you alway, even unto the end of the world."

CHAPTER XLII.

FTER these things Jesus showed himself again to the disciples at the sea of Tiberias: and on this wise showed he himself. There were together Simon Peter, and Thomas called Didymus, and Nathanael of Cana in Galilee, and the sons of Zebedee, and two other of his disciples. Simon Peter saith unto them, "I go a fishing." They say unto him, "We also go with thee." They went forth, and entered into a ship immediately; and that night they caught nothing. But when the morning was now come, Jesus stood on the shore: but the disciples knew not that it was Jesus. Then Jesus saith unto them, "Children, have ye any meat?" They answered him, "No." And he said unto them, "Cast the net on the right side of the ship, and ye shall find." They cast therefore, and now they were not able to draw it for the multitude of fishes. Therefore that disciple whom Jesus loved saith unto Peter, "It is the Lord." Now when Simon Peter heard that it was the Lord, he girt his fisher's coat unto him, (for he was naked,) and did cast himself into the sea. And the other disciples came in a little ship; (for they were not far from land, but as it were two hundred cubits,) dragging the net with fishes. As soon then as they were come to land, they saw a fire of coals there, and fish laid thereon, and bread. Jesus saith unto them, "Bring of the fish which ye have now caught." Simon Peter went up, and drew the net to land full of great fishes, an hundred and fifty and three: and for all there were so many, yet was not the net broken. Jesus saith unto them, "Come and dine." And none of the disciples durst ask him, Who art thou? knowing that it was the Lord. Jesus then cometh, and taketh bread, and giveth them, and fish likewise. This is now the third time that Jesus showed himself to his disciples, after that he was risen from the dead. So when they had dined, Jesus saith to Simon Peter, "Simon, son of Jonas, lovest thou me more than these?" He saith unto him, "Yea, Lord: thou knowest that I love thee." He saith unto him, "Feed my lambs." He saith to him again the second time, "Simon, son of Jonas,

He appears to seven of them by the sea of Galilee.

lovest thou me?" He saith unto him, "Yea, Lord; thou knowest that I love thee." He saith unto him, "Feed my sheep." He saith unto him the third time, "Simon, son of Jonas, lovest thou me?" Peter was grieved because he said unto him the third time, "Lovest thou me?" And he said unto him, "Lord, thou knowest all things; thou knowest that I love thee." Jesus saith unto him, "Feed my sheep. Verily, verily, I say unto thee, When thou wast young, thou girdedst thyself, and walkedst whither thou wouldest: but when thou shalt be old, thou shalt stretch forth thy hands, and another shall gird thee, and carry thee whither thou wouldest not." This spake he, signifying by what death he should glorify God. And when he had spoken this, he saith unto him, "Follow me." Then Peter, turning about, seeth the disciple whom Jesus loved following; which also leaned on his breast at supper, and said, "Lord, which is he that betrayeth thee?" Peter seeing him saith to Jesus, "Lord, and what shall this man do?" Jesus saith unto him, "If I will that he tarry till I come, what is that to thee? follow thou me." Then went this saying abroad among the brethren, that that disciple should not die: yet Jesus said not unto him, "He shall not die"; but, "If I will that he tarry till I come, what is that to thee?" This is the disciple which testifieth of these things, and wrote these things: and we know that his testimony is true.

Then the eleven disciples went away into Galilee, into a mountain where Jesus had appointed them. And when they saw him, they worshiped him: but some doubted. And Jesus came and spake unto them, saying, "All power is given unto me in heaven and in earth."

He appears to them in a mountain in Galilee.

He showed himself alive after his passion by many infallible proofs, being seen of them forty days, and speaking of the things pertaining to the kingdom of God: and, being assembled together with them, commanded them that they should not depart from Jerusalem, but wait for the promise of the Father, "which," saith he, "ye have heard of me." "For John truly baptized with water: but ye shall be baptized with the Holy Ghost not many days hence." When they therefore were come together, they asked of him, saying, "Lord, wilt thou at this time restore again the kingdom to Israel?" And he said unto them, "It is not for you to know the times or the seasons, which the Father hath put in his own power. But ye shall receive power, after that the Holy Ghost is come upon you: and ye shall be witnesses unto me both in Jerusalem, and in all Judæa, and in Samaria, and unto the uttermost part of the earth." And when he had spoken these things, he led them out as far as to Bethany, and he lifted up his hands, and blessed them.

The last appearance of Christ.

And it came to pass, while they beheld, he was taken up: and a cloud received him out of their sight. And he was received up into heaven, and sat on the right hand of God. And while they looked steadfastly

PETER LEAPS FROM THE BOAT TO MEET JESUS.

toward heaven as he went up, behold, two men stood by them in white apparel; which also said, "Ye men of Galilee, why stand ye gazing up into heaven? this same Jesus, which is taken up from you into heaven, shall so come in like manner as ye have seen him go into heaven." And they worshiped him, and returned to Jerusalem with great joy from the mount called Olivet, which is from Jerusalem a sabbath day's journey, and were continually in the temple, praising and blessing God.

The ascension.

And they went forth, and preached everywhere, the Lord working with them, and confirming the word with signs following.

And many other signs truly did Jesus in the presence of his disciples, which are not written in this book, the which, if they should be written every one, I suppose that even the world itself could not contain the books that should be written. But these are written, that ye might believe that Jesus is the Christ, the Son of God; and that believing ye might have life through his name. Amen.

ANALYTICAL INDEX.

Pharisees refuse to admit evidence of miracles, 139.
　as to their being blind also, 141.
　told of raising of Lazarus, 174.
　warn Jesus that Herod would kill him, 161.
　accuse Jesus of receiving publicans and sin-
　　deride Jesus, 170. 　　　　　[ners, 166.
　tempt Jesus, 180.
　command to deliver up Jesus, 188.
　consternation of, at Jesus' miracles, 192.
　seek to lay hands on Jesus, 197.
　　to entangle Jesus in his talk, 198.
　their words but not works to be followed, 202.
　build tombs of prophets, 203.
　conspire against Jesus, 215.
　furnish Judas with men to take Jesus, 232.
　ask Pilate to secure sepulcher, 250.
　　　　See *Elders, Jews, Scribes.*
Philip, brother of Herod, tetrarch of Iturea, 33.
　his wife Herodias married to Herod, 106.
Philip, the Apostle, called, 40.
　one of the Twelve, 68.
　questioned as to feeding multitude, 108.
　Greeks ask, to see Jesus, 214.
　asks Jesus to show the Father, 222.
　　　　See *Apostles, Disciples.*
Phylacteries of scribes and Pharisees, 202.
" *Physician,* heal thyself," 56.
Physician not required by the whole, 64.
Pieces of silver, Jesus betrayed for thirty, 215.
Pigeons, offering of, on purification, 24.
Pilate, Pontius, governor of Judea, 33.
　mingles blood of Galileans with sacrifices, 159.
　Jesus delivered to, 236.
　intercedes for Jesus, 240.
　wife of, sends message about Jesus, 240.
　・ writes a title over Jesus' cross, 244.
　permits securing of sepulcher, 250.
Pillow, Jesus sleeping on a, in a storm, 95.
Pinnacle of temple, Jesus set on a, 36.
Piping, children, in market-place, 85.
Pit, cattle fallen into, on Sabbath, 66, 161.
Pitcher, man carrying a, 215.
" *Place* of a skull," 244.
Plagues cured by Jesus, 82.
　　　　See *Miracles.*
Plain, Jesus on a, 68.
Plant not planted by God rooted up, 116.
Pleasure of the Father in giving the kingdom, 157.
Pleasures of life choke word, 92.
Plow, he who puts hand to, not to look back, 132.
Pool of Bethesda, 51.
　of Siloam, 139.
Poor, the, Jesus sent to preach to, 56.
　blessed, 70.
　inviting, true hospitality, 164.
　charity to, enjoined, 182.
　dedication to, by Zaccheus, 187.
Porch, Solomon's, Jesus in, 160.

Porches of Bethesda, 51.
Possessed. See *Demoniac, Devils, Miracles, Spirits.*
Possible, all, with faith, 126.
　with God, 18, 182.
Pots, washing of, traditions concerning, 115.
Potter's field, bought with betrayal money, 242.
Pounds, parable of ten, 187.
Power given to become sons of God, 15.
　of Elijah (Elias), John Baptist endued with,
　　the Highest to overshadow Mary, 18. [17.
　word of Jesus with, 60.
　to heal, etc., given to Apostles, 68, 103, 146.
　of Jesus to lay down and retake his life, 142.
　faith, 126, 172, 192, 222.
　darkness, 232.
　Jesus to be on right hand of, 236.
　of Pilate only from above, 240.
　to remit sins given to Apostles, 258.
　all, given to Jesus, 262.
Prætorium, the, 240.
Praise of heavenly host at birth of Jesus, 21.
　　　　See *Glory.*
Prayer at time of incense, 17.
　of Zacharias heard, 17.
　Jesus in, 60, 68, 110, 121.
　of Jesus for Peter, 220.
　for the Holy Ghost, 222.
　with his disciples, the last, 228.
　in Gethsemane, 230.
　for those who crucified him, 246.
　for persecutors, 76.
　not to be made for show, 76.
　to be made in secret, 76.
　with faith, 192.
　in the name of Jesus, 226.
　the Lord's, 76, 148.
　for laborers in the harvest, 101, 114.
　joint, promised to be heard, 128.
　temple, the house of, 192.
　of publican and of Pharisee, 180.
　enjoined, 78, 148, 211.
　of obedient will be heard, 224.
　in Jesus' name heard, 222, 226.
　against temptation enjoined, 230.
　of thief on cross, 246.
Preach, the disciples sent forth to, 103, 144.
Preaching of John Baptist, 33.
　of Jesus, 56, 60, 62, 87, 105.
　Jonah (Jonas), 152.
　the Twelve, 103.
　Christ enjoined, 258.
　the Apostles after ascension, 264.
　　　　See *Sermon, Teaching.*
Preparation of children of Israel by John Baptist,
　of ways of the Lord, 22, 33. 　　　[17.
　for the Passover, 215.
　the, 248.
Presentation of Jesus in temple, 24.

www.ingramcontent.com/pod-product-compliance
Lightning Source LLC
Chambersburg PA
CBHW020848020726
47497CB00005B/1309